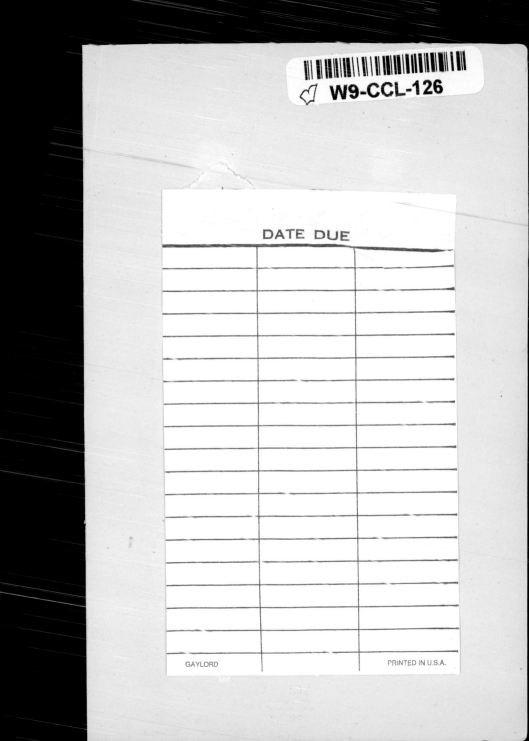

DATE DUE

THE NINE FIRST FRIDAYS

THE NINE FIRST FRIDAYS

FRIDAYS

The 'Great Promise' of the Sacred
Heart of Jesus to Saint Margaret Mary
(*Its origin, authenticity and meaning*)

By
REV. J. O'CONNELL

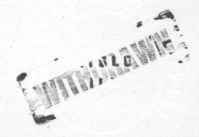

LONDON
BURNS OATES & WASHBOURNE LTD.
PUBLISHERS TO THE HOLY SEE

First published . 1934
Reprinted . . 1935
Second edition . 1949

242.72
018n2

NIHIL OBSTAT:

Edwardus J. Mahoney, S.Th.D.,
Censor deputatus.

IMPRIMATUR:

✠ Joseph Butt,
Vicarius generalis.

Westmonasterii
die 30 Julii, 1934.

MADE AND PRINTED IN GREAT BRITAIN
FOR
BURNS OATES & WASHBOURNE LTD.

28 ASHLEY PLACE, LONDON, S.W.1

TO

THE SACRED HEART

OF JESUS

IN

REPARATION

CONTENTS

FOREWORD

THE devotion of the ' Nine Fridays ' is a very popular act of piety and is now widespread throughout the Church. It consists in going to Holy Communion for nine consecutive first Fridays of the month as an act of love of reparation towards the Sacred Heart of Jesus. When our Divine Lord, in a series of apparitions that took place from 1672 to 1690, at the Visitation Monastery in Paray-le-Monial (France), taught St. Margaret Mary Alacoque the devotion to His Adorable Heart in the form in which it has been received by the Church and is now practised by nearly all the faithful, He revealed to her not only the principles of the devotion, but also particular practices that He wished adopted by lovers of His Sacred Heart. One of these practices was to receive Holy Communion on the first Friday of each month in reparation to the Divine Heart ; this act of devotion was ordered by our Lord in one of the ' great ' apparitions—that of 1674. Later on He taught the Saint another act of the devotion, it was to receive Holy Communion on *nine* first Fridays of the month without a break. So pleasing to the Sacred Heart is this act of devotion that to those who carry it out He has promised the inestimable grace of a happy death.

This is what St. Margaret Mary tells us about the devotion of the ' Nine Fridays ': ' One Friday, during Holy Communion, He [our Lord] said these words to His unworthy servant, if she is not mistaken, " I promise thee, in the exceeding great mercy of my Heart, that Its all-powerful love will grant to all those who will receive Holy Communion on nine consecutive first Fridays of the month, the grace of final repentance, not dying in my disfavour and without receiving their sacraments, [my divine Heart] becoming their assured refuge at the last moment " ' (*Vie et Œuvres*, II, 397).

Our Divine Lord when teaching St. Margaret Mary the devotion to His Sacred Heart made her many promises in favour of those who would practise different acts of the devotion ; but in favour of no practice did He make such a wonderful promise as to those who ' make the Nine Fridays.' Hence this promise is known as ' The Great Promise.'

Many of the pious faithful who ' make the Nine Fridays ' with earnestness and love know little or nothing about ' the Great Promise '—they ' make the Fridays ' because they see other people doing so and because they instinctively realize that the practice is an excellent act of devotion to the Sacred Heart. This little book tries to tell them all about the ' Great Promise '—its origin, its authenticity, its meaning. Many, too, know of the Promise ; they know the wording of it, they accept it as it stands, and they ' make the Fridays ' with simple faith, with a firm hope that the Sacred Heart will give them what He has promised and with an ardent love for Him in return for the ' all-powerful ' love that has made such a promise. This little book aims at confirming such souls in their unquestioning faith, in their unwavering hope, in their trusting love.

Some there are—whether of that little knowledge which is said to be ' a dangerous thing,' or of that great knowledge which is a formidable thing, I know not—who are suspicious about and unfriendly to ' the Great Promise.' They are startled by its greatness ; they are alarmed by the abuses that will arise (they think) from its too simple acceptance ;

they see difficulties, historical or theological, which lead them to question the authenticity of the Promise or, at least, to reject its literal interpretation.

This little book, with great diffidence, endeavours to show that there is no sound reason for questioning the authenticity of the 'Great Promise'; no valid argument against accepting the words of the Promise as they stand and as they are accepted by the simple faithful.

The writer of this booklet hopes that at best he may set doubting minds at rest in reference to the 'Great Promise' and lead to its being preached with even greater confidence and insistence, and so promote the devotion known as 'the Nine Fridays'; that at least he may reawaken interest in the Promise and stimulate fresh inquiry into the credentials of the devotion, so that if these credentials are not trustworthy their weakness should be exposed and thus truth would be attained more fully, and devotion which is unsound or suspect of superstition would be ended or mended.

To attain to truth has been the sole object of the writer of this little book—to try and determine if the 'Great Promise' is really authentic and, if so, what is its true meaning. He has endeavoured to avoid special pleading. He has not consciously suppressed or misinterpreted any fact that would be damaging to his thesis, which is that 'the Great Promise' is authentic and is to be interpreted literally, just as it stands. He has frankly stated every argument which has—to his knowledge—been advanced, or which he himself can suggest against the authenticity or literal interpretation of the Promise, and he has endeavoured to reply to these adverse arguments.

The revelations of St. Margaret Mary as found in her authentic writings are now universally accepted as genuine. If the 'Great Promise' is found among

these revelations, there is a presumption in favour of
its authenticity (why select this particular revelation
for rejection if her other revelations be accepted ?).
It is for those who challenge that authenticity to
offer satisfactory evidence that the ' Great Promise '
is spurious. If the 'Great Promise' is genuine the
presumption is—as in the case of every written statement—that it ought to be interpreted according to the
natural, obvious meaning of the words. It is for those
who refuse to accept the ' Promise ' as it stands to
furnish valid reasons to prove that the ' Promise '
may not be accepted literally.

Devotions which flourish in the Catholic Church
—with at least its tacit approval—are to be credited,
like the faith of the Church, with a reasonable basis,
whether that basis be apparent to the general run of
Catholics or not. In such matters—even apart from
the watchful care of the teaching Church—Catholic
instinct is sound. The practice of devotion which is
known as ' making the Nine Fridays,' and whose
foundation is the ' Great Promise,' is in possession in
the Church—it is widespread, it is very dear to many
if not to all lovers of devotion to the Sacred Heart of
Jesus—it is for those who dislike it or who question
its authenticity to show cause. In point of fact, at
the present day there is scarcely any serious writer
who calls in question the authenticity of the Promise,
and few who positively oppose its literal interpretation ; but there are some who, for no adequate
reason but because they are lacking in knowledge or
simply out of prejudice, are suspicious of the devotion
of the Nine Fridays and sometimes, in a rather
irresponsible way, cast doubts and aspersions on it.

The first chapter of this book, entitled ' St. Margaret Mary,' is a very brief and necessarily quite
inadequate account of two vast subjects—the wonderful life story of St. Margaret Mary and the history

of the origin and development of devotion to the
Sacred Heart. It is merely intended to give readers
the historical setting of the ' Great Promise.'

Many kind friends—some of them known to me
only by correspondence, all with the common link of
an ardent desire to promote the interests of the Sacred
Heart—helped me with this book. From St. Margaret Mary's Convent, the Visitation Monastery of
Paray-le-Monial, I got items of information (such as
variant MS. readings), my MS. was read there and—
a most precious favour—it was placed near the Altar
of the Apparitions, near the body of St. Margaret
Mary and in the room where she died and which is
now a private chapel in the Convent, that it might
receive the blessing of the Sacred Heart together with
the prayers of our Lady of the Sacred Heart, of
St. Margaret Mary and of Blessed Claude de la
Colombière.

My MS. has been read, too, by Père A. Hamon,
S.J. (Rouen), by Fr. C. Lattey, S.J. (Heythrop), and
by three other priests and from these savants I have
received criticisms and suggestions of the greatest
value. To Fr. Lattey's kindness I also owe valu-
able help in research. Dom L. Gougaud, O.S.B.
(Farnborough), kindly read my book in proof. The
Directors of the Apostleship of Prayer all over the
world aided me by replying to a questionnaire about
the practice of the ' Nine Fridays ' in different
countries.

To all these good friends I offer my sincere and
most cordial thanks, and I pray the Sacred Heart to
reward them for their very kind help.

Feast of Corpus Christi (May 31), 1934.

FOREWORD TO THE SECOND EDITION

WHEN this little book was published, it had a very favourable reception, though its subject matter is a controversial one. It has been for some years out of print and now a second edition is called for. Nothing that has been written about the first edition has necessitated even the smallest change in the text.

J. O'CONNELL.

May 1948

BIBLIOGRAPHY

THE original and chief sources of information on the revelations made by the Sacred Heart of Jesus to St. Margaret Mary are contained in *Vie et Œuvres de Sainte Marguerite-Marie Alacoque*, published by the Monastery of the Visitation of Paray-le-Monial after the third edition by Monseigneur Gauthey, Archbishop of Besançon (3 vols., 1920, J. de Gigord, 15 Rue Cassette, Paris).

These volumes contain the autobiography, letters and other writings of the Saint ; her Life written by two of her contemporaries of the Visitation Monastery ; the memoirs of her superiors and her sisters of Paray-le-Monial and other writings connected with the life and revelations of St. Margaret Mary. They are derived from the original MSS. or from very early copies. They were first published by the nuns of the Visitation Monastery of Paray in 1867 and another edition in 1876. Then Monseigneur Gauthey—chaplain at Paray, Vicar-General of the diocese of Autun, Bishop of Nevers and finally Archbishop of Besançon—collaborated with the Visitation Monastery and edited a more critical and augmented edition, and this appeared in 1915. A still more perfect edition was subsequently prepared and appeared in 1920, the year of the canonization of St. Margaret Mary, after the Archbishop's death (1918). The three volumes of *Vie et Œuvres* (2332 pp.) place at the disposal of writers on devotion to the Sacred Heart the archives of the Monastery of Paray-le-Monial and of other Visitation Convents in so far as they have any bearing on the subject.

Throughout this book *Vie et Œuvres* is quoted as *V.O.*

Other books which directly deal with the devotion of the Nine First Fridays (the ' Great Promise ') are :

ALOISI-MASELLA, P. (S.J.).—*I Primi Venerdì del Mese* (Messaggero del Sacre Cuore, Roma, 1931).

BAINVEL, J.-V. (S.J.).—(i) *Devotion to the Sacred Heart* (translated from the fifth French edition by E. Leahy. Burns Oates and Washbourne, 1924).

(ii) Article ' Cœur Sacré de Jésus,' in *Dictionnaire de Théologie Catholique* (Vacant), Vol. III (i), 1911.

BEGASSIÈRE, R. DU BOVAYS DE LA—Article ' Cœur de Jésus,' in *Dictionnaire Apologétique de la Foi Catholique* (1909).

BOUBÉE, JOS. (S.J.).—*Les Promesses du Sacré-Cœur* (1921).

BOUDINHON, A.—'Les Neuf Premiers Vendredis,' in *Revue du Clergé Français*, 1903, Vol. XXXVI.

CATHREIN, VIKTOR (S.J.).—*Die Verheissungen des göttlichen Herzens.* (Herder, 1919.)

ESTÉBANEZ, M. G. (S.J.).—*La Grande Promesse du Cœur de Jésus* (translated from the Spanish. Beauchesne, Paris, 1913).

GALEAZZI, D. (S.J.).—*De Præcipuo e Promissis SS. Cordis Jesu.* (Desclée, Roma, 1910.)

HAMON, A. (S.J.).—(i) ' Les Vies de la Bienheureuse Marguerite-Marie Alacoque,' in *Études*, 1902, Vol. XCI.

(ii) ' Le Texte de la Grande Promesse du Sacré-Cœur,' in *Études*, 1903, Vol. XCV.

(iii) ' La Bienheureuse Marguerite-Marie,' in *Études*, 1904, Vols. XCIX and C.

(iv) *Histoire de la Dévotion au Sacré-Cœur* (4 vols. to date, Beauchesne, Paris, 1923–1931).

HATTENSCHWILLER, J. (S.J.).—*Die grosse Verheissung des göttlichen Herzens Jesu* (Innsbruck, 1923).

LE BACHELET, X.-M.—(i) ' La Grande Promesse du Sacré-Cœur,' in *Études*, 1901, Vol. LXXXVIII.

(ii) Review of Fr. Galeazzi's book in *Études*, 1911, Vol. CXXVI.

McDONNELL, J. (S.J.).—*The Promises of the Sacred Heart.* (Burns Oates & Washbourne, 1913.)

NIX, H. J. (S.J.).—*Cultus SS. Cordis Jesu.* (Herder, Friburg, 1905.)

O'LOAN, D.—' The Nine Fridays,' in *Irish Ecclesiastical Record*, 1895, Vol. 16 (p. 543).

PETROVITS, J. C.—*Devotion to the Sacred Heart*. (Herder, 1918.)

RAMIÈRE, H. (S.J.).—' La Grande Promesse du Cœur de Jésus,' in *Le Messager du Cœur de Jésus*, 1883, Vol. XLIII.

'SACERDOS.'—' A Ground of Hope' (The 'Great Promise'), in *The American Messenger of the Sacred Heart*, Feb. 1898.

THURSTON, H. (S.J.).—' The Nine Fridays,' in *The Month*, June 1903.

TRUPTIN, E.—*Les Promesses du Sacré-Cœur à Sainte Marguerite-Marie*. (Tequi, Paris, 1924.)

VERMEERSCH, A. (S.J.).—(i) 'La Grande Promesse du Sacré-Cœur,' in *Le Messager*, Jan. 1903.

(ii) 'La Grande Promesse,' in *Études*, 1903, Vol. XCV.

(iii) *Pratique et Doctrine de la Dévotion au Sacré-Cœur* (2 vols., Casterman, Paris, 1922).

These works are referred to throughout this book by the name of the author alone.

B

THE
NINE FIRST FRIDAYS

CHAPTER I

ST. MARGARET MARY (1647–1690)

THAT great lover of Jesus, the chief apostle of devotion to His Sacred Heart, Margaret Alacoque, was born on July 22, 1647, in the village of Lautecour (called nowadays Les Janots) in the diocese of Autun in Burgundy, the daughter of Claude Alacoque—a judge and royal notary—and Philiberte Lamyn. She was the fifth of a family of seven, having three brothers and a sister older than herself and one sister and one brother younger. Three days after her birth she was baptized in the parish church of Verosvres. From her tenderest infancy Margaret was a child of divine predilection and our Lord surrounded her with His love, watchful that from the earliest moment her heart should belong entirely to Him. Of happy disposition, naturally gay, impressionable and very intelligent she showed, even as a small child, a marked horror of sin and a great love of purity. When but a tiny child of four, moved by an impulse of divine grace, she made a vow of perpetual chastity without—as she afterwards confessed—even knowing the meaning of the words which she uttered. When but a little more than eight years old she lost her father and was placed under the care of the Urbanist nuns (a branch of the Poor Clares) at Charolles and there made her first Communion at the age of nine (1656). God destined her for a life of great suffering and this began when she was only eleven years old. She was afflicted with some form of rheumatism or paralysis which confined her to her bed for nearly four years, obliging her to leave school and return home. Perhaps the great devotion of her early age was devotion to our Blessed Lady and only when she made a vow to become one of Mary's daughters did she recover her health. She was then fourteen. Her home life was made very unhappy by the persecution which she and her mother suffered at the hands of some of her father's relatives and already as a child she trod the path of humiliation—a path she was to know so well in later years. Even as a child, too, she attained the highest degree of contemplation in prayer and practised much mortification. She had a remarkable devotion to the Blessed Sacrament which grew daily greater and from the tabernacle our Lord taught her the value of the cross, giving her, side by side with great suffering, immense consolation (as she relates in her autobiography). Even before her eighteenth year she had that ardent desire to suffer that was later such a marked feature of her convent life. Over a long period she was the victim of a cruel interior struggle. She desired to become a religious, but she feared her own unworthiness and she was pressed by her mother to marry. To solve her doubts she added to much ardent prayer the practice of the most severe penance and at last, in her twentieth year, God ended her hesitation and she determined, cost what it may, to enter a convent. Victory was not, however, yet attained as her mother and eldest surviving brother, Chrysostom, offered a strenuous opposition to her designs. In 1669, at the age of twenty-two (at the time Confirmation was given only at long intervals in that region), she was confirmed and added to her baptismal name, Margaret, the name of Mary. Having hesitated for some time between the Ursulines and the Visitandines, Margaret Mary chose the Order of the Visitation of our Blessed Lady, which had been founded in the opening years of the seventeenth century by St. Francis de Sales and St. Jane Frances de Chantal. On June 20, 1671, she entered the convent of Paray-le-Monial, a convent that had been opened on a first Friday of the month, September 4, 1626. She was clothed on August 25, the feast of St. Louis of France, in the year of her entry, and from the very beginning of her religious life was in the most intimate communion with our Lord. He made Himself her spiritual director and granted her, when she was still but a novice, the most extraordinary graces and favours, developing in her a deep love of Him and a remarkable attachment to suffering.

In 1672, Mother Marie-Françoise de Saumaise became the superior of the monastery of Paray. She it was who was destined to mould, under our Lord's guidance, the religious life of Margaret Mary for six years, to become her devoted friend and confidante and to receive from her the immortal revelations of Jesus Christ concerning devotion to His Sacred Heart. Though a perfect novice, she was not admitted to profession at the end of her year's novitiate, since some of her community did not approve of the fact that there was something out of the ordinary, known to them in a vague way, in her life. However, this difficulty was overcome and on November 6, 1672, she was professed. During her retreat in preparation for this event, began the wonderful favour that our Lord conferred on Margaret Mary of His 'actual and continual' presence with her and the opening for her of His wounded side as her ' actual and perpetual dwelling.' Her love of the Blessed Sacrament grew daily more ardent and it was in the presence of the Most Holy Sacrament exposed for adoration that the ' great ' apparitions of our Lord took place.

Before Christ's revelations to Margaret Mary she knew but little, if anything, of devotion to the Sacred Heart. She may have learned something of it from the writings of St. Gertrude or St. Francis de Sales, but it was from the lips of our Lord Himself that she was to learn the inmost secrets of this devotion and was to receive His command to teach it to the world in the form in which it has since been recognized and approved by the Church. Our Lord prepared the humble Visitandine for His marvellous revelations not only by granting her a high and ever-growing degree of holiness, but also by frequent visions in which He showed her His Heart, both directly and by different allegorical representations, and taught her Its love. By slow degrees—step by step only— our Lord, from 1672 until her death (1690), made known to this beloved soul the inestimable riches of His Sacred Heart and taught her how men were to know, love and honour It. This He did especially by the ' great ' apparitions of 1673, 1674 and 1675, in which the ' great ' revelations were made.

The first of the ' great ' apparitions took place on the feast of St. John, the Apostle, December 27, 1673. While praying before the Blessed Sacrament our Lord appeared to St. Margaret Mary and caused her to rest for a long time on His divine breast (as St. John had done at the Last Supper), ' when He discovered to me,' she wrote later, ' the wonders of His love and the inexplicable secrets of His Sacred Heart, which He had always hidden from me until He now opened It to me.' Speaking to the Saint, Christ said, ' My divine Heart is so inflamed with love

for men, and for you especially, that, no longer being
able to keep within Itself the flames of Its burning
love, It must needs spread them abroad through
you, and make Itself known to men in order to
enrich them with Its precious treasures which I
unfold to you. . . . I have chosen you (He added)
as an abyss of unworthiness and ignorance for the
accomplishment of this great purpose that all may be
done by me.' Our Lord then took Margaret Mary's
heart and placed it in His own, where she saw it as
a tiny atom which was consumed in this blazing
furnace, and then withdrawing it like a burning flame
He replaced it in her body. ' As a sign,' He told her,
' that the great favour that I have just accorded to
you is not imaginary and that it is the foundation of
all those graces which I shall confer on you, although
I have healed up the wound in your side, the pain
will remain always ; and if hitherto you have taken
only the name of my slave, I give you now the title of
the beloved disciple of my Sacred Heart.'[1]

After this first ' great ' revelation of December 27,
Margaret Mary received many others in which the
Sacred Heart showed Itself more and more to her
and made gradually clearer Its eternal designs. Each
first Friday of the month It showed Itself to the saint
as a sun shining with a dazzling light. In one of these
apparitions, in 1674, ' this divine Heart was presented to me on a throne of fire, more brilliant than
the sun and clear like a crystal, with this adorable
wound, and it was surrounded with a crown of thorns,
which meant the piercing that our sins had inflicted
on It, and a cross above It, which meant that from the
first moments of His Incarnation, that is from the
time when this Sacred Heart was formed, the cross
was planted in it. . . . And He made me see that the
ardent desire which He had of being loved by men

[1] *V.O.*, II, 70, 71 (Autobiography).

and of withdrawing them from the path of perdition, into which Satan was driving them in crowds, had made Him plan to show His Heart to men, with all the treasures of love, of mercy, of grace, of holiness and of salvation which It contained. . . . That this devotion [to the Sacred Heart] was as a last effort of His love with which He would favour men in these latter ages.'[1] Our Lord added that He wished 'the Heart of God' honoured under the likeness of this heart of flesh and He desired the picture of His Heart to be venerated, and He promised many favours to those who would comply with His wishes.

On another occasion during the year 1674, when the Saint was kneeling in prayer before the Blessed Sacrament exposed, our Lord appeared to her 'shining in glory with His five wounds gleaming like five suns, and from His sacred humanity flames burst forth on every side, but especially from His adorable breast which was like a furnace, and this having opened He showed me His all-loving and all-lovable Heart, which was the living source of these flames.'[2] Christ then spoke of His love for men and of the ingratitude and coldness which He received in return, and He ordered the Saint to make reparation by receiving Holy Communion on the first Friday of each month and on each Thursday night to spend the hour from eleven to midnight prostrate on the ground in prayer, sharing in the sadness which our Lord suffered in the Garden of Olives.

Following these apparitions Margaret Mary suffered from a burning fever and grew well only when her superior ordered her to seek a cure from our Lord. He granted her prayer and our Lady herself came and healed the Saint.

[1] Letter to Fr. Croiset (Nov. 3, 1689), (V.O., II, 571).
[2] V.O., II, 72 (Autobiography).

Towards the close of 1674 our Lord informed Margaret Mary that He was about to send her a director. It was Fr. Claude de la Colombière, S.J. (1641–1682)—now Blessed Claude (1929)—who was then at Lyon but was appointed superior of the Jesuit house in Paray in February 1675. Being the extraordinary confessor at the Monastery of the Visitation he met Margaret Mary for the first time when he went to hear confessions on the Ember days (March) and a few days later, by order of her superior, Mother de Saumaise, the Saint manifested her conscience to him and gave him an account of her intimate relations with her Divine Master. Not yet, however, it would seem, did she speak of the devotion to the Sacred Heart. Fr. de la Colombière, a holy priest and prudent director, was destined by Divine Providence to be the first great helper of Margaret Mary in making known and loved the Sacred Heart. Yet only after many interviews with him, only after a vision in which it was shown to her that Fr. de la Colombière was to have a great part in the propagation of the devotion, only after a direct command of our Lord (given in the apparition of June 1675), did Margaret Mary speak to her confessor of the Sacred Heart and bid him on the part of our Lord to do his utmost to establish the devotion to that adorable Heart.

On one of the days within the octave of the feast of Corpus Christi, June 1675, took place what is considered the greatest of all the apparitions. St. Margaret Mary was before the Blessed Sacrament and was receiving from God ' exceeding great graces of His love.' Our Lord showed her His Heart and said : ' Behold this Heart which has so loved men that It has spared Itself nothing even to being exhausted and consumed to prove to them Its love ; and in return I receive from most men only ingratitude, by their irreverence and sacrileges and by the coldness and contempt they show towards me in this sacrament of love. But what is still more painful to me is that it is hearts which are consecrated to me that treat me so. It is on that account that I ask that the first Friday after the octave of the Holy Sacrament be dedicated as a special feast to honour my Heart by communicating that day and by making an act of reparation to atone for the insults which It has received during the time that It has been exposed on the altars. I promise thee also that my Heart will open wide to spread abundantly the influence of Its divine love on all who will give It this honour and induce others to do so.'[1] Our Lord then commanded Margaret Mary to seek the aid of Fr. de la Colombière in establishing the devotion to the Sacred Heart.

While our Lord continued until the end of her life (1690) to favour His servant with many apparitions and to make clearer and clearer to her the nature of devotion to His Heart and the favours and rewards that He had in store for those who would honour it, the apparition of June 1675 marks the end of the ' great ' apparitions and revelations. Of these nothing, or practically nothing, was then known in the convent at Paray except to the superior (Mother de Saumaise) and to Fr. de la Colombière, and he ordered St. Margaret Mary not to speak of them. In July 1676 the Saint's mother died, and two months later she was deprived of her director and friend Fr. de la Colombière, when he left Paray for London, whither he was sent as preacher to the Duchess of York (Mary of Modena, the wife of the future James II). In June 1678 her friend and confidante, Mother de Saumaise—who had tested the Saint severely in

[1] The Saint wrote the account of this apparition to Fr. de la Colombière. It is found in his *Œuvres Complètes* (VI, pp. 118 *sqq.*), and in *V.O.*, I, 137 (Contemporaines).

many ways during her six years as superior and who
was now satisfied as to the genuine character of the
revelations that had been made to Margaret Mary—
was recalled to Dijon and was succeeded by Mother
Peronne-Rosalie Greyfié, from the head house of the
Order at Annecy. Some time after her arrival our
Lord commanded Margaret Mary to write a will
making Him the heir to all the good that she would
do during life and to the suffrages which would be
offered for her after her death. She wrote and signed
this will—and so did Mother Greyfié as witness—on
December 31, 1678. In return Christ made her ' the
heiress of His Heart and of all Its treasures,' promising her that she would be wanting in aid only
when His Heart would be wanting in power.

Our Lord had frequently warned the Saint that
she must become a victim for His glory and so from
the year 1678 to 1684 she was in constant suffering of
body and soul, but she bore her cross with the greatest
patience and resignation.

Having been banished from London in December
1678, Fr. de la Colombière called at Paray on his
way to Lyon in February 1679 and saw Margaret
Mary once. Two and a half years later—in the
autumn of 1681—he returned to Paray, sick unto
death. He saw the Saint at least twice—for the last
time in October—and he died on February 15, 1682,
at Paray, where our Lord wished him to offer the
sacrifice of his life, as He revealed to St. Margaret
Mary.

Twice during the term of office of Mother Greyfié
was the Saint cured for a definite period from her
almost constant ill-health on requesting a cure from
our Lord at the order of her superior, but when she
ceased to suffer in body her sufferings of soul increased. Frequently she gave evidence of possessing
prophetic power and of a knowledge of the secrets of

the world beyond the grave, telling, for example, the moment when certain persons (including Fr. de la Colombière) passed from Purgatory to Heaven.

In May 1684 Mother Greyfié finished her work at Paray. She was a woman of remarkable sanctity, discernment and prudence, a superior of the highest order. She, like Mother de Saumaise, had been the confidante of Margaret Mary, and she had tried her even more severely than her predecessor. She left Paray convinced of the sanctity of Margaret Mary and of the truth of her revelations, of which she had been assured by Fr. de la Colombière before his death. She was succeeded by Mother Marie-Christine Melin, one of the Paray community, who at once chose Margaret Mary as her assistant. Some months later (January 1685) the Saint was made mistress of novices and took charge of the novitiate of the Visitation of Paray, within whose walls the first public act of the devotion to the Sacred Heart as revealed to Margaret Mary was to take place.

On the Friday following the Octave of Corpus Christi—the day chosen by our Divine Lord for the future feast of His Sacred Heart—the Saint attached to an altar in the novitiate a pen-and-ink sketch of the Heart of Christ and she and her novices, it would seem, paid it honour. When her feast day—the feast of St. Margaret, July 20—came, the novices as a surprise for their beloved mistress erected a little altar, decorated it as well as they could, and enthroned on it this picture of the Sacred Heart. The Saint was filled with joy and she and each novice consecrated herself to the Divine Heart. An invitation to the professed sisters to come and join in the devotion was refused. The older nuns resented the introduction of what they considered a novelty in devotions and they complained to Mother Melin. She censured Margaret Mary and her novices for their

zeal and prohibited the introduction of the devotion
outside the novitiate, but permitted it within its
walls. She also forbade the Saint the making of the
first Friday Communion, as Mother Greyfié had in
1678 forbidden her the hour of prayer on Thursday
night, and as she had been punished for this by the
death of one of her community,[1] so Mother Melin
was punished by the grave illness of one of the sisters
—an illness which was cured only when the superior
consented to allow the Saint's Communion.

Our Lord, however, was moving slowly but surely
towards the accomplishment of His designs and the
vindication of His faithful servant. In January 1686,
Mother Greyfié, now superior at Semur, had an
image of the Sacred Heart exposed in the oratory of
her convent and she sent small pictures, showing the
Heart as It had been revealed to St. Margaret Mary,
for some of the sisters at Paray. On June 21, the
Friday after the octave of Corpus Christi, to the
intense joy of the Saint, the devotion to the Sacred
Heart which a year before had been rejected as a
novelty, was definitely adopted in the community at
Paray. The nuns there had been much impressed by
Mother Greyfié's act and still more so by the publication of the Spiritual Retreat of Fr. de la Colombière
in which he had spoken of the devotion and of the
revelations, hence their gradual change of heart.
Sister Marie Madeleine des Escures, the nun who
had first refused the invitation of 1685 to come to the
novitiate and take part in honouring the Divine Heart,
set up an altar in the community chapel, placed on it a
miniature of the Sacred Heart that Mother Greyfié
had sent to Margaret Mary, and invited the professed sisters to come and venerate it. All, moved
by a special impulse of grace, agreed to do so and the
nuns decided that a special chapel should be built in

[1] Cf. Contemporaines (*V.O.*, I, 166).

the convent grounds to enshrine a large image of the Sacred Heart—a great triumph for the prayers and sufferings of St. Margaret Mary.

In 1687 the Saint was again appointed assistant and remained in this office until her death (1690). As time went on she did more and more by her letters and conversations to make known and loved the devotion to the Sacred Heart and, to her intense joy and consolation, she saw it take root and slowly begin to grow, at first in the Visitation monasteries at Dijon (through Mother de Saumaise), at Semur (by the efforts of Mother Greyfié) and at Moulins at the instance of Mother de Soudeilles. Through the zeal of this superior the first booklet on the devotion was drawn up and printed at Moulins in the autumn of 1686 and a copy sent to Paray and to Dijon. In this convent of Dijon Sister Jeanne-Madeleine Joly wrote Litanies and a Mass in honour of the Sacred Heart, which the confessor of the convent corrected and translated into Latin, and her superior (Mother Desbarres) tried to secure approbation for them in Rome. The petition for approval was referred back to the bishop of the diocese (Langres). Through his Vicar-General, and later personally, the Bishop gave his approbation and early in 1689 the first book on the devotion for public use was published ; while in February of that year the first Mass in honour of the Sacred Heart was celebrated in the convent at Dijon.

Meanwhile, on the feast of the Visitation, July 2, 1688, St. Margaret Mary had a vision in which the Heart of Christ appeared on a throne of flame and by It were our Lady, St. Francis de Sales, and Fr. de la Colombière, while all around were religious of the Visitation Order, accompanied by their guardian angels. Our Lady explained to the Saint that the Visitation nuns and the Fathers of the Society of Jesus were constituted the special apostles of devo-

tion to the Sacred Heart.   This choice of our Lord
was confirmed by another vision which the Saint had
in May (or June) 1689.   Only after much hesitation
and when many obstacles had been overcome, did
these two religious bodies, years after the death of
Margaret Mary, fully accept the commission which
had been given them through her.   Longer still was
the hesitation of the Church itself in the official
acceptance and promulgation of the devotion to the
Heart of Jesus as it was revealed to the Saint of Paray.

In two letters to Mother de Saumaise in 1689,
Margaret Mary explained a remarkable message that
she had been bidden by our Divine Lord to send to
Louis XIV, King of France, concerning the promotion of devotion to the Sacred Heart.   It would seem
that the message never reached the King; if it did he
ignored it.

At this time the Saint suffered sorely in body, but
she was recompensed by many heavenly joys and
favours, and she was much consoled by the slow but
certain development of the devotion to the Sacred
Heart, despite suspicion, opposition and many
obstacles.   In word and by letter she continued her
ardent apostleship of the love and worship of the
Divine Heart and she was most active in openly
promoting the devotion during the last years of her
life.   She interested in it Fr. François Froment, S.J.
(who was in Paray from 1688–1695), and induced him
to write a book to explain and defend the devotion,
but this did not appear until 1699 at Besançon.
Early in 1689 she got in touch with a young Jesuit—
Jean Croiset—who was doing his theological studies
at Lyon and began a remarkable correspondence with
him in the April of that year.   She was directed by
him in spiritual matters and in turn gave him direction.   She made him the confidant of her momentous
secrets—writing to him at great length—and he

became an ardent apostle of devotion to the Sacred Heart. At her instance and with her full approval he published in the early summer of 1689 a book entitled *La Devotion au Sacré-Cœur de notre Seigneur Jésus-Christ,* which was widely diffused. The relations between Fr. Croiset (he was ordained in the spring of 1690) and the Saint had the formal and repeated approval of our Divine Lord, and Margaret Mary told the young priest that he had been chosen to know, love and honour the Sacred Heart in a very special way and to spread devotion to It. In December 1689 Fr. Croiset journeyed to Paray to see St. Margaret Mary, whom he had not previously met, and then returned to Lyon confirmed in his zeal for the devotion.

The last months on earth of Margaret Mary were peaceful and she manifested in them again and again her remarkable gift of prophecy and her great power in obtaining marvellous favours from God. She grew weaker and weaker in health and spoke of her approaching death, which she desired, not only because of her longing to go to her Divine Master, but also because she felt—she knew—that the continuance of her life was now but an obstacle to the progress of devotion to the Sacred Heart. In truth, only after the death of His intimate friend and faithful servant could the secrets of Christ's dealings with her be revealed to the world.

On October 8, 1690, began the Saint's last illness. She contracted a fever which was, however, light, and it was thought that there was no danger of death. She knew otherwise, and the day before her death she received Holy Communion with the intention of receiving It as Viaticum—knowing that she would never again receive her Beloved under the sacramental species—though there was no apparent sign of death. In her last hours God once again sent the cross of keen spiritual suffering, as He had sent it so often before, but this was succeeded by a heavenly peace and calm. On the evening of Tuesday, October 17, between seven and eight, she died in the arms of Sisters Françoise Rosalie Verchère and Peronne-Rosalie de Farges (as she had foretold years before), while being anointed.

Through the zeal of Mgr. Jean Languet, one time ecclesiastical superior at Paray, then Bishop of Soissons, and later Archbishop of Sens, the diocesan examination of her life was begun in 1715, twenty-five years after her death. More than a century, however, passed before the cause of Margaret Mary—delayed by the hatred of the Jansenists for devotion to the Sacred Heart and the storm which they raised against it—was taken up in Rome, and only on March 30, 1824, did Leo XII instruct the Congregation of Sacred Rites to proceed to the examination of her life (the Apostolic Process). In 1827 (by decree of September 22) the Congregation declared her writings free from anything that was 'worthy of theological censure,' as the technical phrase goes, and in 1844 the examination of 'her virtues and other supernatural favours' was begun. By decree of April 24, 1864, Pius IX confirmed the truth of three miracles that had been examined in proof of the heroic sanctity of Margaret Mary, and on September 18 she was beatified by that great Pope. The cause of her canonization was resumed two years later, but only on January 6, 1918, was the examination of two further miracles approved and the decree determining her canonization was signed on March 17. On the feast of the Ascension, May 13, 1920, Margaret Mary Alacoque was solemnly canonized—proclaimed a saint—by Benedict XV and her feast fixed on October 17, the date of her death. In 1929 (June 26) the celebration of her feast was extended to the Universal Church.

c

St. Margaret Mary was destined by God for a mission of the most sublime order, she was to be the attentive and faithful disciple of our Lord Himself and then the intrepid apostle and authorized evangelist of devotion to His Sacred Heart—of this devotion in the form that was revealed to her by Christ and that was later to be accepted and approved by His Church and practised by the faithful throughout the world.

Devotion to the Sacred Heart, in one form or another, was known long before the time of St. Margaret Mary. Traces of it can be found from the eleventh century. Its sources were twofold : by some of the saints it was received by direct revelation—for example, SS. Gertrude and Mechtilde (in the thirteenth century), St. Catherine of Siena (fourteenth), St. Frances of Rome (fifteenth), St. Peter Canisius (sixteenth) learned it in their intimate relations with our Lord—by others it was reached through meditation on the Passion, leading to special devotion to the Five Wounds and particularly to the wound in the Side of Christ. In this way devotion to the Heart of Jesus is found in the lives of such saints as St. Anselm (eleventh century), St. Bernard (twelfth), St. Bonaventure and St. Clare (thirteenth), Blessed Angela of Foligno (fourteenth), and of many of the ascetics and mystics from the twelfth to the seventeenth century. Devotion to the Sacred Heart, in different forms, also appeared in some of the great Religious Orders—the Benedictines and Franciscans (from thirteenth century), the Dominicans (fourteenth), the Carthusians (fifteenth), the Jesuits (sixteenth)—before the days of the Saint of Paray-le-Monial. The devotion reached its greatest extension—before the revelations to St. Margaret Mary—in the seventeenth century, especially through the wonderful labours of St. John Eudes (1601–1680), who obtained for devotion to the Hearts of Jesus and Mary liturgical recognition (within the boundaries of his own congregations) and was such an ardent lover and zealous preacher of this devotion that he has been styled by Pius X (who beatified him) and Pius XI (who canonized him) the creator of this liturgical cult of the Hearts of Jesus and Mary and ' a father, a doctor, and an apostle ' of the devotion.

Yet it would seem that the many manifestations of devotion to the Sacred Heart, in its various forms, before the time of St. Margaret Mary, had scarcely any influence on our present devotion.[1] Though the flame of devotion to the Divine Heart had been enkindled in the eleventh century, it had burned rather fitfully, sometimes blazing forth with an almost startling brilliancy, in certain places and at certain times, only to die down again, though never to become quite extinct. Veneration of the Heart of our Lord remained to the time of St. Margaret Mary the private devotion of certain privileged souls—at most of certain religious bodies or dioceses. It assumed various forms and sometimes was not well defined in its object and often not clearly distinguished from devotion to the Five Wounds. The revelations of Paray changed all this slowly but surely. Through them the devotion—in the form in which it has been accepted by the Church, and is now universally practised—was definitely learned[2] and manifested, devotion to the living Heart of Christ, the Heart of flesh, inseparably united to the Divine Person of the Word, as a symbol of the interior life of Jesus Christ, but especially of His love for men, a love forgotten, despised and outraged. By the revelations St. Margaret Mary was taught also how the devotion was to be practised and how it was to be

[1] Cf. Hamon, *Histoire*, II and III, *passim* ; *Le Christ* (1932), pp. 711 *sqq.* ; Bainvel, 127 *sqq.*   [2] Cf. pp. 59 *sqq.*

propagated. Above all (and it is this that makes St.
Margaret Mary quite different from all the earlier
lovers of the Sacred Heart) the Saint was given *a
mission*, a mission to the entire world, a mission to
teach the devotion, to proclaim the promises of our
Lord to all who would practise and promote it, a
mission to propagate the devotion and to draw souls
to Christ by means of it, a mission to make devotion
to the Sacred Heart a *Catholic* devotion.[1]

St. Margaret Mary was prepared from infancy by
our Lord Himself for her mission of disciple and
apostle of devotion to His Adorable Heart. First He
prepared her by her natural character, she was intelligent and noted for her prudence and common sense,
but she had little education in the ordinary sense of
the word and her revelations began when she was a
young nun just out of the novitiate and of no account
in the eyes of her contemporaries, so that (as our
Lord explained to her), the divine hand in her mission
could not fail to be recognized. ' I have chosen thee,'
said Christ, ' as an abyss of unworthiness and
ignorance for the accomplishment of this great design
[to make known the treasures of the Divine Heart] so
that all may be done by me.'[2] Especially did our
Lord prepare Margaret Mary by making her a saint
and by endowing her in a marvellously high degree
with those virtues which her mission particularly
required—obedience, simplicity, humility, love of
suffering. These were to be irrefutable testimony to
her sincerity and to the truth of her revelations.
He favoured her, too, with extraordinary supernatural gifts—the grace of His ' continual and sen-

[1] This mission has been recognized by many official documents
of the Church, e.g. in the brief of beatification (1864), and the bull
of canonization (1920) of St. Margaret Mary, in the Encyclical Letter
Annum Sacrum of Leo XIII (1899) on the consecration of mankind
to the Sacred Heart.
[2] *V.O.* (Autobiography), II, 70.

sible' presence, the gift of foreknowledge or of a
knowledge of things beyond the grave, the power to
obtain favours in a miraculous way. Then He
taught her the devotion to His Sacred Heart—
revealing it very gradually to her in a series of apparitions which began shortly after her religious profession (1672) and, it would seem, lasted to the end
of her life (1690)—and explained to her the ways in
which He desired that it should be practised,[1]
making clear to her that above all He sought a love of
reparation in return for His boundless but despised
love for men.

Next our Lord selected those who were to aid the
Saint in her mission—Fr. de la Colombière, S.J.,
Mother de Saumaise, Mother Greyfié, Fr. Croiset,
S.J., and later the Order of the Visitation and the
Society of Jesus—and bade her convey to them His
commands. Then came the revelation of His promises in favour of those who would practise and
promote the devotion[2]—promises designed to draw
men and to induce them to adopt the devotion.
Lastly He made known to St. Margaret Mary that
His graces and favours were given not for herself
only but for others too. In spite of her great reluctance to make known her revelations (for more than
ten years they were known only to her superiors and
spiritual directors) Christ ordered her to publish to
the world the treasures of His Sacred Heart—
' treasures of love, of mercy, of grace, of sanctification, of salvation.'[3] She must be an instrument of
our Lord to draw souls to Him, a canal of graces which
she was to distribute in a generous way, for this
had Christ prepared her from her youth.[4] ' I have

[1] There is no evidence that before the revelations St. Margaret
Mary knew anything of devotion to the Sacred Heart. (Cf. Hamon,
Histoire, III, pp. 270, 286.)

[2] See pp. 22 sqq.   [3] Letter to Fr. Croiset (1689), V.O., II, 572.
[4] V.O., I, 460 ; II, 92, 94, 193, 582 et passim.

chosen you' for this mission, were the words of our
Lord often repeated.[1] By our Lord Himself, then,
was Margaret Mary given a formal, authentic mission to proclaim the devotion to the Sacred Heart
and to make it—in due time and by ways designed by
Him—a devotion of the Catholic Church.

The Saint began her direct apostolate only after
the death of Fr. de la Colombière (1682) and the
publication of his *Spiritual Retreat* (1684), which for
the first time gave some information concerning the
revelations of Paray, and she began it in the novitiate
of her convent (1685). Only after her own death,
at the early age of forty-three (1690), could her
mission be fully realized by making known to the
world the full story of her life and her wonderful
revelations.

Our own times have witnessed the complete
triumph of the mission of St. Margaret Mary. The
Church, having first officially recognized and sanc-
tioned devotion to the Sacred Heart as taught by St.
Margaret Mary, by a decree of Clement XIII in
1765, gave it special commendation through Pius
IX in 1875, and in the Encyclical Letter, *Annum
Sacrum*, of Leo XIII in 1899. At the beginning of
this century Leo XIII consecrated the entire world
to the Sacred Heart, confirming the fact that devotion to the Sacred Heart had indeed become a
devotion of the Catholic Church, and this consecration is now renewed yearly by order of Pius X
and of Pius XI on the feast of Christ the King.[2]
Benedict XV canonized the Saint of Paray in 1920,
thus confirming her sanctity and the truth of her mission. Pius XI, in 1928, issued his Encyclical *Miserentissimus Redemptor*, on the duty of reparation to the
Divine Heart, and then raised the feast of the

---

[1] e.g. *V.O.*, II, 70 (cf. Hamon, III, 271).
[2] Encyclical Letter, *Quas primas* (1925).

Sacred Heart—which had first secured official recognition in the Sacred Liturgy in 1856 and had gradually been elevated in rank since then—to the highest place of honour, making it a first-class feast with a privileged octave. It is the devotion of the apparitions of 1673, 1674 and 1675 that is epitomized in the new prayer of the feast :

' O God, whose mercy deigns to lavish upon us infinite treasures of love in Thy Son's Heart, wounded by our sins, grant, we pray Thee, that we may offer Him devout homage, loving service, and fitting reparation : through the same Jesus Christ, Thy Son, our Lord, who is God living and reigning with Thee in the unity of the Holy Spirit, for ever and ever. Amen.'

CHAPTER II

THE PROMISES OF THE SACRED HEART

A REMARKABLE and distinctive feature of devotion to the Sacred Heart is to be found in the promises which our Lord made to St. Margaret Mary in favour of those who would practise and promote the devotion. God has always dealt with men in a way consonant with their nature—by drawing them to do His will by promises of reward. It was so in His dealings with the chosen people under the old dispensation; it was the way of Christ in the new, promising even a hundredfold return for compliance with His desires. And so it is in the history of the revelation and propagation of devotion to the Sacred Heart. 'That men might the more readily respond to that wonderful and overflowing desire of love,' wrote Leo XIII, in his Encyclical, *Annum Sacrum* (1899), on the devotion, 'Jesus, by the promise of rich rewards, called and drew all men to Him'; and the Church, in the Divine Office[1] on the feast of St. Margaret Mary (October 17), recalls the order which Christ gave to the Saint to see that public worship was given to His Heart, 'promising great rewards from the treasures of Heaven.'

St. Margaret Mary, in her writings, insists again and again on the ardent desire of Christ to pour out blessings with a royal generosity on those who would honour His Sacred Heart and return Him love for love. Relating in her Autobiography her great

[1] Matins, Lesson V.

reluctance to write down—as her spiritual directors had ordered—an account of her relations with our Lord, she tells of her complaining to Him and of His insistence that she should do as she had been ordered. Explaining to her His reasons why she should write, He said : ' In the second place [I wish you to write] to teach you that you must not appropriate these graces [i.e. the profusion of graces with which He had enriched her], nor be niggardly in distributing them to others, since I wish to use your heart as a channel to pour out these graces according to my plans into souls, several of whom will thus be drawn from the abyss of perdition, as I shall show you later. And in the third place to make you see that I am Eternal Truth who cannot lie—*I am faithful to my promises*—and that the graces that I have bestowed on you may undergo every form of scrutiny and test.'[1]

In a letter to Mother de Saumaise (in August 1688)—following the failure of efforts in Rome to obtain approval of the text of a Mass and Litanies in honour of the Sacred Heart[2]—the Saint relates that when she complained to our Lord of this check to the spread of the devotion, He replied : ' Why are you grieved about that which shall be for my glory ? For at the present time I am loved and honoured on no other ground than that of Providence and of love itself, and that is very pleasing to me ; but this ardour can grow cold . . . and when it does, I shall rekindle this fire in hearts with all these privileges and with even greater ones. . . .'[3]   In the early revelations to St. Margaret Mary the promises were first adumbrated and then stated in general terms, e.g. ' great rewards ' ; in the later revelations of her last years

---

[1] *V.O.* (Autobiography), II, 35.   The *Contemporaines* (see p. 29) quote this passage in their Life of the Saint (*V.O.*, I, 62).

[2] Cf. Hamon, *Histoire*, I, 395 *sqq.*

[3] Letter XCI (*V.O.*, II, 413).

(1685–1690), following the ' great ' apparitions (1673–
1675), they were made by Christ in a much more
definite form.[1] Sometimes our Lord's promises were
in favour of individuals (e.g. Mother de Saumaise,
M. Greyfié, M. Melin, Fr. Croiset, S.J.) who helped
on the devotion to the Sacred Heart, at other times in
favour of all who adopted the devotion or of certain
classes (e.g. priests, religious communities, sinners).
Sometimes the promises favoured those who in
general adopted or promoted the devotion, at other
times they were a reward for a particular act of the
devotion (e.g. for the celebration of the feast of the
Sacred Heart, for honouring Its image, for making the
Nine First Fridays). In some promises the reward
is general (e.g. special protection, an abundance of
the gifts of Christ's Heart), in others a special one
(e.g. peace, the power to touch hardened hearts, the
grace of final repentance).

The promises are found scattered through the
writings of St. Margaret Mary ; they are often
repeated and in different forms (e.g. in her letters
to Fr. Croiset she recapitulates them), and many
of them are chronicled in the earliest ' Lives ' of her
(e.g. in Fr. Croiset's *Life*). At quite an early date,
when exactly is not known, lists of these promises,
extracted from the MSS. of the Saint's writings, were
drawn up and were circulated in books or leaflets.[2]
The earliest French lists contain eight promises,
many later lists (especially those in English) contain
twelve,[3] others, again, have sixteen (e.g. Truptin's [4]

---

[1] Cf. Hamon, *Histoire*, I, 379 (note) ; Bainvel, 50.

[2] Cf. Bainvel, 49 ; Truptin, 5 ; McDonnell (pp. 9–10 and p. 152)
suggests that lists of the promises were circulated, e.g. in the diocese
of Autun, shortly after the death of St. Margaret Mary (lists which
included the ' Great Promise '), but gives no authority for his
view.

[3] Hence English-speaking people know the ' Great Promise ' as
the ' Twelfth Promise.'   [4] Cf. p. xvii.

list). It is merely a matter of division and arrangement[1]—thus the promise numbered 3 in the French
list ' *pour les personnes séculières* ' really contains
the first six promises of the list giving twelve. All
the promises which are usually given in these lists,
and others also, *are* found in the writings of St.
Margaret Mary, though they are not always stated
quite accurately in the leaflets (in which they are
given in an abbreviated form), and the really correct
lists are those that give the exact words of each
promise as set down by the Saint herself. Thus in
the latest list (1920) from Paray itself, in leaflet
form, the promises are given in the exact words of
St. Margaret Mary (with references given to *Vie et
Œuvres*) and with a guarantee from the diocese of
Autun that the version is authentic.

Towards the end of their Life of St. Margaret Mary
the *Contemporaines*[2] write : ' She had such a lively
faith in the promises which she had received from
Jesus Christ concerning the establishment of this
devotion [to the Sacred Heart] that she said with
conviction to Fr. de la Colombière, when all seemed
opposed and there was little appearance of its ever
being received, that, when she would see everyone
strongly opposed to [*déchaîné contre*] this same
devotion, she would never despair of seeing it established, since she had heard these words of her
Saviour, " I shall reign despite *my* enemies and I
shall accomplish the plan for which I have chosen
you, whatever the efforts of those who would thwart
it." '[3]

That the various promises were made to St.
Margaret Mary by our Lord, that she correctly

---

[1] In the list containing eight Promises the ' Great Promise ' is
number seven ; in the longer list it is the twelfth, and so is often
known as the ' Twelfth Promise.'

[2] See p. 29.   [3] *V.O.*, I, 275.

recorded them, and that her account of them has reached us substantially unchanged—all that is a matter of historical evidence. No more proof can reasonably be required for the historic truth of events that concern the direct relations between God and men or for the historical authenticity of statements that embody the promise of supernatural favours, no less proof should be accepted by prudent persons, than for the historical validity of other events, or statements. Among the promises made to St. Margaret Mary is the celebrated promise known as the Twelfth, or 'Great' Promise.

With the historical authenticity of the 'Great Promise' alone is this book concerned, and we shall now show that there is excellent historical evidence that the 'Great Promise' was made to St. Margaret Mary, that she recorded it correctly, and that her account of it has come down to us intact and unchanged.

CHAPTER III

THE chief sources of our information about the life and revelations of St. Margaret Mary are her own writings and the early ' Lives ' of her that were written. The more important writings of the Saint are :

(1) *Le Petit Mémoire des Grâces reçues :*[1]

Mother de Saumaise was Superior of the Visitation Monastery of Paray-le-Monial from 1672–1678, and on November 6, 1672, received the profession of Margaret Mary Alacoque. Six months later she ordered the Saint to write an account of her interior life. This was begun in April 1673, and Margaret Mary wrote it from time to time, relating the graces she received between 1672 and 1678—the first years of her religious life and the years of the ' great ' apparitions. The *Contemporaines* inserted most of this memoir in their ' Life ' of the Saint. It was fully published, for the first time[2]—from MS. 6,[3] with the variants noted, the autograph is not extant—by Archbishop Gauthey in his editions (1915 and 1920) of *Vie et Œuvres.*[4]

(2) *Mémoire or Autobiography :*

This is an account of her life which St. Margaret Mary wrote about 1685, by order of her then spiritual director, Father Rolin, S.J. The autograph is extant. The Saint wrote it with great reluctance

---

[1] *V.O.*, II, 121 *sqq.*   [2] *V.O.*, II, 9.
[3] See p. 34.   [4] See p. xv.

and only from obedience. It seems that she ceased to write it after the departure of Fr. Rolin from Paray (1686) and so this account of her life is unfinished.[1] She herself kept the MS. and on her death-bed desired Sister de Farges to burn it, but was persuaded by this sister, with great difficulty, to leave it intact in the keeping of the superior. It was published for the first time by Fr. Galliffet, S.J., in 1733, in his book on devotion to the Sacred Heart. The authentic text was not, however, given to the public until *Vie et Œuvres* was issued in 1867, and a more accurate text has been provided in the Gauthey editions of 1915 and 1920.

(3) *Letters :*[2]

The latest editions of the *Vie et Œuvres* published one hundred and forty-two letters of St. Margaret Mary, written between 1678 and 1690. Of forty-eight of these the autographs are extant. The others are published from (*a*) copies found in early MSS.— written shortly after the Saint's death, at the end of the seventeenth and beginning of the eighteenth centuries[3]—of which there are six or seven ; (*b*) a very exact and literal translation of them made into Italian at Rome in 1828–9, for the use of the Roman authorities in connection with the process for beatification of St. Margaret Mary.[4] The translation was made from copies of the letters officially certified as authentic by the episcopal chancellary of Autun. These letters are written mostly to members of the Visitation Order (especially to Mother de Saumaise— to whom forty-eight of them are addressed—to Mother Greyfié and to Mother de Soudeilles), some to the Ursulines, some to her brother (Chrysostom),

---

[1] *V.O.*, II, 27.   [2] *V.O.*, II, 209 *sqq*.
[3] Cf. *V.O.*, I, 339 ; II, 6, 12, 516, 633.
[4] Cf. *V.O.*, I, 339 ; II, 10, 214.

and ten, long and important letters, to Fr. Croiset, S.J.[1] It was in a letter written to Mother de Saumaise at Dijon, between 1687 and 1689, that St. Margaret Mary gave the account of the ' Great Promise.'

While some of the letters were quoted by early biographers of the Saint (e.g. Languet, Galliffet, Croiset), most of them were not published until the Visitation Monastery of Paray issued *Vie et Œuvres* in 1867.

The second great source of information about St. Margaret Mary and her revelations is the early ' Lives ' of her which were written : [2]

(1) *The Contemporaines :*

The name *Contemporaines* is given to two sisters of the Visitation Monastery of Paray—Sisters Françoise-Rosalie Verchère and Peronne-Rosalie de Farges—who had been novices of St. Margaret Mary, and in whose arms she died.[3] Immediately after her death these nuns began to collect the material for her ' Life,' and it was written by the hand of Sister Verchère. It was begun in 1690 or 1691,[4] and not quite complete in 1713,[5] but finished by 1715. The original MS. is extant. The Life was based on the Saint's autobiography, on her letters and other writings, on the memoirs of Mother de Saumaise and Mother Greyfié, on the *Abregé* of Fr. Croiset,[6] and on the personal knowledge of the *Contemporaines*, of Margaret Mary—a very intimate knowledge—and

[1] See p. 30.
[2] Other important sources are memoirs of Mother de Saumaise and Mother Greyfié, and the sworn evidence of the contemporaries of St. Margaret Mary which was given at the diocesan process of 1715 (see p. 15). These, however, have no direct connection with the ' Great Promise ' and so are omitted.
[3] See p. 15.
[4] Cf. *V.O.*, I, 33 and 298 *note ;* Hamon, *Études*, 1902 (vol. 91), p. 722 ; Galeazzi, 19.
[5] *V.O.*, I, 298 *note.*   [6] See p. 30.

that of others of her contemporaries. This Life was not at first published, but it was placed at the disposal of Mgr. Languet when he was asked by the Convent of Paray, in 1715, to write a Life of the Saint.[1] The Life of the *Contemporaines* was not published until 1867, when *Vie et Œuvres* was issued from Paray. It contains an account[2] of the ' Great Promise,' quoting, apparently, from the letter of Margaret Mary to Mother de Saumaise.

(2) *Father Croiset's ' Life '* (1691) :

In the last year of her life (1689–1690), St. Margaret Mary got in touch with a young Jesuit Father, then at Lyon, Fr. Jean Croiset.[3] She made known to him that he was very dear to the Sacred Heart, that he shared in a special way in Its treasures of grace, and that our Lord destined him to be a great apostle of devotion to His Divine Heart. At the Saint's instance, Fr. Croiset wrote a book on the devotion (which was not published until 1691, after Margaret Mary's death, but she read and approved the greater part of it), and she wrote him during the last year of her life, a number of long letters (ten of them are extant) in which she gave an account of her revelations and taught him the devotion to the Sacred Heart. When his book appeared he had added to it a Life of the Saint—*Abregé de la Vie d'une Religieuse de la Visitation Sainte-Marie*—the first published Life of Margaret Mary Alacoque.

(3) *Archbishop Languet's ' Life '* (1729) :

In 1729 appeared *La Vie de la Vénérable Mère Marguerite-Marie, Religieuse de la Visitation Sainte-Marie*, by Mgr. Languet. Languet had been Vicar-General of the diocese of Autun and ecclesiastical superior of the Monastery of Paray. It was he who, as delegate of the Bishop of Autun, began, in 1715,

---

[1] See *infra*.　　[2] *V.O.*, I, 261.　　[3] Cf. p. 13.

the diocesan process for the beatification of Margaret Mary. Subsequently he became Bishop of Soissons and then (1731) Archbishop of Sens. His Life, which was begun about 1715, but not completed until 1729, is based chiefly on the Life of the *Contemporaines* (then completed in MS.), on the writings of Margaret Mary and on the evidence of her contemporaries (given under oath at the diocesan process).[1] In this Life an account of the 'Great Promise' is given.[2]

[1] Père Hamon remarks (*Études*, 1902, Vol. 91, p. 729) that for a century and a half writers on St. Margaret Mary copied or abridged Languet's Life ; only at the period of her beatification (1864) was fresh work done in the examination of her life.

[2] Cf. p. 37.

D

CHAPTER IV

THE TEXT OF THE 'GREAT PROMISE'

THE first relation of the 'Great Promise' was given in a letter written by St. Margaret Mary to Mother de Saumaise at Dijon. Mother de Saumaise was the great friend and confidante of the Saint to whom she opened her mind most fully and freely; she had been superior at Paray from 1672–1678, during the period of the 'great' apparitions, and the first to learn Margaret Mary's wonderful secrets. Later on, when she had left Paray, the Saint made known to her in several of her letters[1] that she had been chosen by our Lord to take the place of Fr. de la Colombière (after his death in 1682), as the helper of Margaret Mary in the work of teaching and propagating the devotion to the Sacred Heart, and that God destined for her extraordinary graces. Mother de Saumaise was the chief correspondent of St. Margaret Mary.

The date of the letter in which the 'Great Promise' is related—letter 86 in the latest edition of *Vie et Œuvres*—is given by Archbishop Gauthey as '[mai] 1688'; *Annales du Monastère de Dijon* (p. 146), cites a fragment of the letter and gives it as subsequent to February 1689; the Roanne MS. of Paray (known as MS. 'D.')[2] affixes to the letter the date '168,' with a fourth figure that is illegible and might be

---

[1] e.g. Letters XLI (*V.O.*, II, 306), LV (*ib.*, 337), LXXXIX (*ib.*, 408), and cf. *V.O.*, III, 272.   [2] See p. 35.

either ' 9,' or ' 7.'[1] It suffices to know that the letter was written between 1687 and 1689.

Nowhere else in her writings does St. Margaret Mary refer to the 'Great Promise,' but this is not surprising since—it would seem—the revelation was made to her not long before her death (1690), and subsequently to almost all that she wrote. The original letter is lost—neither the autograph of *any* of the forty-eight letters which the Saint wrote to Mother de Saumaise, nor the autograph of the *Petit Mémoire*[2] which was also addressed to her is extant. The originals were sent to Mother de Saumaise at Dijon (where she was superior after her period of office at Paray), and it is usually said[3] that they perished there at the time of the French Revolution, but the autographs of the letters to Mother de Saumaise may have perished at quite an early period, for at the diocesan process for the beatification of St. Margaret Mary which began in 1715, only copies of these letters were produced,[4] while the originals of all other letters then extant (others have since been discovered) were forthcoming—with the exception of one letter which had been written to Sister Joly, written to Dijon also. In a note to the *Contemporaines*,[5] Archbishop Gauthey remarks that ' since the period at which the *Contemporaines* wrote, all the originals of the letters to Mother de Saumaise have disappeared, save one alone,[6] of which the autograph is preserved at the Visitation of Rennes,' and not at Dijon. Possibly Mother de Saumaise destroyed the originals

---

[1] Cf. Hamon, *Études*, 1903, Vol. 95, p. 854. Father Hamon in *Histoire*, I (1923), p. 434, note 2, says that 1687 seems to him the more probable date of the letter.

[2] See p. 27 and cf. *V.O.*, I, 335.

[3] E.g. Hamon, *Études*, 1903, p. 854; Galeazzi, 4; Vermeersch, 131.

[4] *V.O.*, II, 14.   [5] *V.O.*, I, 95.

[6] Letter LV (*V.O.*, II, 337).

before her death (1694),[1] especially as Margaret Mary
in many of her letters to this religious begged, as
she did in letters to others, that they might be destroyed.[2]   At all events at whatever period the
autographs disappeared, we have faithful early copies
of them.   In their Life of the Saint, the *Contemporaines* speak of having made a faithful copy of the
letters to Mother de Saumaise.[3]   In 1715, but twenty-
five years after the death of Margaret Mary, and in
the lifetime of many of her correspondents, the then
superior of Paray, Mother de la Garde, presented
(under oath) for the diocesan process, amongst
other writings of the Saint, an extract of twenty-
seven letters, '*tiré fidèlement sur les originaux*,' which
had been addressed to Mother de Saumaise.[4]   Among
these was the letter in which the account of the ' Great
Promise' occurs.   These early copies which were
presented at the diocesan process have been preserved
intact.[5]

The old collections of MSS. in the archives at
Paray which contain the writings of St. Margaret
Mary, are classified under the numbers 3, 6, 7, 8, 9.
Of these 6 is the largest and most important.   It is
also the most authoritative.[6]   It dates from the
beginning of the eighteenth century.[7]   It contains
particularly all the writings of St. Margaret Mary
which were preserved by Mother de Saumaise, which
were found after her death (1694), ' and which were
copied *from the originals* which are at Dijon.'[8]   (These

---

[1] But see note 8 *infra*.   Nothing is as yet known for certain as to
the date of the loss of these autographs.

[2] Cf. Hamon, *Histoire*, I, 192 ; *V.O.*, I, 331–2.

[3] *V.O.*, I, 95, § 80.   [4] *V.O.*, I, 479.   [5] *V.O.*, II, 217.

[6] *V.O.*, I, 335 ; II, 9. Fr. Hamon, however (I, 10), does not
think so. He prefers MS. " D."

[7] *V.O.*, I, 339.

[8] These words, indeed, suggest that the originals *were* after all at
Dijon after the death of Mother de Saumaise.

words appear on MS. 6.)[1] In addition, MS. 6 is in the writing of Sister Peronne-Rosalie de Farges, one of the two nuns who collected the materials for the Life by the *Contemporaines*.[2] Letter 86 (the one which contains the 'Great Promise') is found in MS. 6 (128), and also in MSS. 3 (5), 8 (43), and 9 (23). It is according to the text of MS. 6 that the letter is given by Archbishop Gauthey in *Vie et Œuvres* (1920), Vol. II, p. 397, and the variant readings from the other MSS. are noted at the foot of the page.

In 1902, Fr. A. Hamon, S.J., discovered at Roanne, in the library of M. Déchelette, a MS. containing some of the letters of St. Margaret Mary.[3] This MS. Gauthey has called 'D.' He considers it of equal authority with the other MSS., but believes MS. 6 to be of greater authority (a view which Fr. Hamon does not accept). In this MS. ' D ' the text of the ' Great Promise ' is also found.

We also have the text in the *authentic* MS. of the Life of St. Margaret Mary by the *Contemporaines*,[4] quoted, apparently, from the letter of St. Margaret Mary, but whether from the original or from a copy is not at present known.

The text appears, too, in the official translation of the Saint's writings into Italian, which was made at Rome, 1828-9, for the Congregation of Sacred Rites. Lastly, an account of the ' Great Promise '—not a quotation, but a statement of the author—appears in Languet's Life of St. Margaret Mary (1729, bk. VIII, pp. 241-2).[5]

While the various texts of the Promise, i.e. the text as given in MSS. 3, 6, 8, 9, D, in the *Contemporaines*, and in the Italian translation—all differ

---

[1] Cf. *V.O.*, II, 9 ; Galeazzi, 16-17.
[2] See p. 29.
[3] *V.O.*, II, 11 ; Hamon, *Études*, 1903, Vol. 95, p. 855.
[4] *V.O.*, I, 261.   [5] See p. 37.

slightly in wording from one another,[1] it is a remarkable thing that *there is not the slightest difference in meaning between them.* Accordingly, which of the versions is really the original one, which of the MSS. is the older or more authoritative are questions which do not concern us in the examination of the ' Great Promise,' seeing that the various versions have exactly the same sense. An examination of the chief versions which are printed on pages 36a and 36b will show this.

Fr. Hamon, S.J., writing in *Etudes* (1903, p. 855), considers that the text of the Roanne MS. (MS. ' D ') most resembles Margaret Mary's style. Thus it is characteristic of her—(*a*) to begin sentences with *et*, (*b*) to use long sentences with present participles (*ne mourant*), and (*c*) to omit the repetition of the subject (the words *mon divin Cœur*, of MS. 6, are omitted in the text of MS. ' D '). Archbishop Gauthey in general prefers[2] MS. 6 to all other MSS., even to MS. ' D,' yet in this particular case a comparison of the texts of the 1867 and 1876 Paray editions (*Vie et Œuvres*) with Gauthey's editions of 1915 and 1920 (see opposite) will show that the Archbishop in giving the text that seemed to him the best has come nearer a good deal to the text as given in MS. ' D.'[3]

---

[1] The Latin version of the Promise which is given in the Bull of canonization of St. Margaret Mary (*Acta Apostolicæ Sedis*, 1920, p. 503) does not agree exactly in wording with any of the old texts, but, of course, the meaning is precisely the same.

[2] *V.O.*, II, 12.

[3] Since writing the above I have discovered (from Paray) that the words *mon divin Cœur* do not occur in MS. 6 (nor in MSS. 3, 8, 9), though they are given in *V.O.* (II, 398). This confirms Fr. Hamon's view of the value of the text of the ' Great Promise ' as given in MS. ' D.'

Letter to Mère de Saumaise.

(I) Ms. 6.	(II) Ms. D (Roanne).
Un jour de vendredi, pendant la sainte communion, il dit ces paroles à son indigne esclave, si elle ne se trompe : ' Je te promets, dans l'excessive miséricorde de mon Cœur, que son amour tout-puissant accordera à tous ceux qui communieront neuf premiers vendredis des mois, de suite, la grâce de la pénitence finale, ne mourant point dans ma disgrâce et sans recevoir leurs sacrements [mon divin Cœur][1] se rendant[2] leur asile assuré au dernier moment.' (*Vie et Œuvres*, 1920, II, 397, Letter LXXXVI.)	Et un jour de vendredi, pendant la sainte communion, il fut dit ces paroles à son indigne esclave, si elle ne se trompe : ' Je te promets, dans l'excessive miséricorde de mon Cœur, que son amour tout-puissant accordera à tous ceux qui communieront neuf premiers vendredis des mois, de suite, la grâce de la pénitence finale, ne mourant point en sa disgrâce, ni sans recevoir leurs sacrements [,] se rendant leur asile assuré en ce dernier moment.' (*Etudes*, vol. 93, 1903, pp. 854 *sqq.*)

(III) Life by *Contemporaines*.	(IV) Authentic Italian Translation.
' Une autre fois, il me semble qu'il me fut dit, après la sainte communion : ' Je te promets, dans l'excès de la miséricorde de mon Cœur, que son amour tout-puissant accordera à tous ceux qui communieront neuf premiers vendredis de chaque mois, tout de suite, la grâce de la pénitence finale, ne mourant point dans ma disgrâce, ni sans recevoir leurs sacraments et qu'il se rendra leur asile assuré, cette heure dernière.' (*Vie et Œuvres*, 1920, I, 261.)	' Un giorno di venerdì in tempo della santa Comunione, Egli (Gesù) disse queste parole alla sua indegna schiava, se non s'inganna : ' Io ti prometto nell' eccessiva misericordia del mio Cuore, che l'amor suo onnipotente accorderà a tutti coloro iquali si comunicheranno per nove mesi continui il primo Venerdì d'ogni mese, la grazia finale della penitenza, e non morranno in disgrazia mia, nè senza ricevere i Sagramenti ; e il mio Cuore sarà per essi un asilo sicuro negli ultimi momenti.' (Galeazzi, p. 10.)[3]

Note.—There are small differences in wording—none whatever in meaning—between the texts of MS. 3, 8, 9 and the texts given above (the version of MS. 3 is almost identical with that of MS. D).

[1] See note 3, p. 36.   [2] MS. 8 has ' promettant de se rendre ' ; all the others (3, 9 and D) have ' se rendant.'

[3] This Italian version is not in exact (verbal) conformity with any of the French versions in the extant MSS.

(V) Latin Version.

Dominus Jesus autem hoc sermone suam fidelem sponsam alloqui dignatus est : ' Tibi polliceor, in profusa mei Cordis misericordia, si qui per novem continentes menses, singulis sextis feriis quoquo mense primis occurrentibus, sacratissimam mensam adeant, omnipotentem Cordis mei amorem pœnitentiæ finalis beneficium eis concessurum: in offensa apud me haud ipsi morientur neque sanctis non exceptis sacramentis ; ac, in postremis illis momentis, tutum eis asylum Cor meum præbebit.'

(Bull of Canonization of St. Margaret Mary
—*Acta Apostolicæ Sedis*, 1920, p. 503.)

TEXT OF THE 'GREAT PROMISE'

(Comparison of the texts of the different editions of *Vie et Œuvres*.)

Letter to Mère de Saumaise.

Vie et Œuvres (Vol. II) Paray editions of 1867 and 1876.	*Vie et Œuvres* (Vol. II) Gauthey's editions of 1915 and 1920.
(1) ' du mois, tout de suite . . .' (2) ' la grâce finale de la pénitence ; . . .' (3) ils ne mourront point en sa disgrâce ni sans recevoir. . .'	' des mois, de suite, . . .' ' la grâce de la pénitence finale,' ' ne mourant point dans ma disgrâce et sans recevoir . . .'
(p. 159.)	(p. 397.)

Life by the *Contemporaines*.

Vie et Œuvres (Vol. I) Paray editions of 1867 and 1876.	*Vie et Œuvres* (Vol. I) Gauthey's editions of 1915 and 1920.
(1) ' les premiers vendredis, neuf mois de suite, . . .' (2) ' qu'ils ne mourront point dans ma disgrâce, . . .'	' neuf premiers vendredis de chaque mois, tout de suite, . . .' ' ne mourant point dans ma disgrâce, . . .'
(p. 291.)	(p. 261.)

CHAPTER V

THE HISTORICAL AUTHENTICITY OF THE ' GREAT PROMISE '

THAT the ' Great Promise ' was known soon after the death of St. Margaret Mary (1690) is evident, for (i) the *Contemporaines* embodied the Promise in their Life of the Saint (which was begun immediately after her death and finished certainly before 1715), during the lifetime of many of the Saint's contemporaries ; (ii) the letter which contains the Promise must have been produced at the informative process in 1715, among the twenty-seven letters to Mother de Saumaise—' faithfully copied from the originals ' —then brought forward,[1] since under oath the superiors of the Visitation Order had to produce all the writings of the Saint that were then known ;[2] (iii) Mother de Soudeilles (who died in 1714), the Superior of the Visitation Monastery of Moulins, began with her community in January 1714, the Nine First Fridays ;[3] (iv) Mgr. Languet, in his Life of St. Margaret Mary—which was begun in 1715,[4] though not published until 1729—speaks as follows of the devotion : ' In another letter she [Margaret Mary] prescribes a practice to honour the Heart of Jesus Christ *which was familiar to her*,[5] and which our

[1] *V.O.*, II, 14 ; I, 479.
[2] Cf. the sworn statement of Mother de la Garde at the diocesan process (*V.O.*, I, 476–7).
[3] *Circulaire de Moulins* (*V.O.*, III, 477, and cf. Hamon, *Études*, 1903, p. 857).   [4] Cf. *V.O.*, I, 34.   [5] Italics are ours.

Lord had suggested to her, leading her to hope for
the grace of final repentance and that of receiving the
sacraments of the Church before dying, for those
who would observe it. It was to make a novena of
Communions for this intention and to honour the
Heart of Jesus Christ, making each of these Communions on the first Friday of the month for nine
consecutive months.'[1]

The *Contemporaines* must have been satisfied
about the authenticity of the Promise when they
quoted it textually in their Life of St. Margaret Mary[2]
(whether from the original letter or from an early
copy of it, or from verbal information from the
Saint we do not know) ;[3] the Visitation superiors
must have believed that letter 86 to Mother de
Saumaise was genuine, or they would not have produced it at the 1715 process (especially as the Promise
itself was calculated to raise difficulties for the cause
of beatification which they had at heart) ; Mgr.
Languet, too, must have been satisfied as to the
authenticity of the letter—and he had excellent
sources of information, the contemporaries and earliest
biographers of the Saint—since he included an
account of the ' Great Promise ' in his Life. When
this book was published (1729) the greatest outcry
was raised against it by the Jansenists and other bitter
opponents of the devotion to the Sacred Heart—a
devotion which was then in its infancy and which was
to become established and recognized by the Church
(in the form in which it had been revealed to St.
Margaret Mary) only in the teeth of fierce opposition

---

[1] *La Vie de la Vénérable Marguerite-Marie*, bk. VII, pp. 241-2.
This account of Mgr. Languet is dealt with on p. 94 ; it is quoted
in Nicollet, *Le Parfait Adorateur du Sacré-Cœur de Jésus* (Paris,
1761), p. 112.
[2] Mother Greyfié, the superior of Paray from 1678 to 1684, to
whom this Life was submitted in 1714, approved of it as correct
(cf. *V.O.*, I, 334 ; Bainvel, 8).   [3] Cf. Estébanez, p. 8.

and after the most mature and long-continued consideration on the part of the Holy See. There is
every reason to believe that the authentic character
of the devotion of the Nine First Fridays would have
been immediately challenged had there been good
ground—or, indeed, any fair reason—for casting
doubt upon it. As Mgr. Languet had the best of
reasons for avoiding anything that would raise
opposition to the devotion to the Sacred Heart (he
was so timid that he even counselled that the Autobiography of St. Margaret Mary should not be
published),[1] it would certainly have been in his
interest to omit any reference to the practice of the
Nine First Fridays, if he doubted the genuine character of the devotion.

When the writings of St. Margaret Mary were
submitted to the Holy See (1819–1827) for examination in connection with the process for beatification,
a copy of letter 86 (the one that contains the ' Great
Promise ') was among them—it was the eighteenth[2]
in a collection of twenty-seven authentic letters
addressed to Mother de Saumaise—and an Italian
translation of it was made.[3] This letter would not
have been sent to Rome unless it were believed
genuine, especially as the Promise was calculated to
raise difficulties—and in point of fact, did ;[4] it was
accepted at Rome as one of the Saint's writings.

The ' Great Promise ' is a very definite promise—
set forth in very precise and exact terms—it is not a
vague, general promise ; it is found in extant documents which are historically known to be faithful
early copies of a letter of St. Margaret Mary. It is
historically absurd to suggest that the Promise was
invented in the lifetime of many of the contemporaries
of the Saint, and that it passed unchallenged both

[1] *Archives de Paray-le-Monial* (cf. Hamon, IV, 80).
[2] Galeazzi, 18.   [3] Cf. pp. 28 and 63.   [4] Cf. p. 96.

by the friends and enemies of the devotion to the Sacred Heart. In point of fact, the opponents of the 'Great Promise' have produced no evidence that such a thing happened.

Objections have been raised on historical grounds to the authenticity of the 'Great Promise,' and these must now be considered.

Objection I. There is only one authentic source of information about the 'Great Promise,' i.e. the letter of 1687 (or 1689) of St. Margaret Mary to Mother de Saumaise (letter 86). The autograph of that letter has been lost, and we know it only in copies. We have evidence that the early copyists of the writings of the Saint, e.g. the *Contemporaines*, Archbishop Languet, Fr. Croiset were inaccurate and unreliable in their work,[1] and so we cannot be satisfied that we have now the real text of the 'Great Promise.'

Reply : We have abundant material for a satisfactory examination of the work of the early copyists of the writings of St. Margaret Mary—material from which it is possible to draw sound conclusions—for we have (*a*) the authentic (original) text of the Life by the *Contemporaines*, and in it they quote extensively from the Autobiography of the Saint *of which the autograph is extant*, and from her letters, *of some of which the autographs are extant ;* (*b*) MS. copies of certain letters of the Saint of which we have also the autographs. Accordingly, we can determine whether the early copyists quoted accurately and, if not, in what way they made modifications. Having learned how they treated documents of which the originals are extant, we can reasonably conclude that they treated others, the originals of which are not now available, in the same way. An examination of the work of the copyists shows that, living in an uncritical age, an age in which it was considered quite

[1] Cf. *V.O.*, I, 11 ; II, 6 *sqq.*

the correct thing to ' improve ' the documents which were copied, they often abridged writings and frequently corrected faults of language and (as they conceived it) faults of style in the Saint's writings, but *they never modified any essential idea, nor changed any clear fact, nor added to the text.* They are invariably found to be faithful in giving at least the *exact thought* of the documents of which we now have the originals.

In the writers of the early Lives of St. Margaret Mary, e.g. Languet, Croiset, we find that the thoughts of the Saint are produced with substantial accuracy ; where there is any departure from exactitude it is the direction of *weakening* the thought of the writer—e.g. by adding, at times, such qualifying phrases as ' *ce me semble*,' and ' *pour ainsi dire*,' when these do not occur in the original—and not in the direction of adding to it. The early biographers sometimes modified the language of the originals—it was the uncritical fashion of the eighteenth century—and sometimes they watered down the thought[1] (being influenced by their surroundings, the vehement opposition to the new devotion to the Sacred Heart, the denunciation of the Saint as a visionary, the ridicule which was poured out on her and her writings), but they did not invent new ideas and give them as St. Margaret Mary's, nor did they change her thought in substance.[2]

In regard to the ' Great Promise ' while we have versions of it that differ, they differ only in wording. There is not the slightest difference between them in thought. The Promise is so definite in character, so precise in its terms and in its conditions—about

[1] There is a remarkable example of this in Mgr. Languet's account of the ' Great Promise ' itself (see p. 94)

[2] Cf. Fr. Hamon's articles in *Études*, 1902 (Vol. 91), pp. 721 *sqq.*; 1903 (Vol. 95), p. 855 ; Bainvel, pp. 13 and 14 ; Thurston, *The Month*, 1903, p. 642.

which all the versions are in complete agreement—
that it does not lend itself to any indeliberate substantial change. ' Jamais,' writes Fr. Hamon[1] (the
greatest modern authority on the literary remains of
St. Margaret Mary), about the copyists and early
biographers, ' en présence de faits bien positifs
comme : *une communion, neuf premiers vendredis,
la pénitence finale, leurs sacrements,* je ne les ai trouvés
en défaut.' Hence there is no valid ground for
believing that the versions of the ' Great Promise '
which we have do not faithfully give the thought of
St. Margaret Mary.

Objection II. St. Margaret Mary herself is strangely
silent about the ' Great Promise,' of which she
speaks only once. It would seem that she attached
little importance to it, or, perhaps, was doubtful
about it.

Reply. (i) The Saint wrote very little after the time
that she first speaks of the ' Great Promise ' (not
earlier than 1687, and perhaps as late as 1689, but a
year or so before her death). Besides, the ' Great
Promise,' important as it is, is but one small item of
the devotion to the Sacred Heart, and to the Saint
was given the immense task of teaching and propagating the entire devotion—a devotion familiar to us
now, but at that period almost unknown. We could
not reasonably expect her, in such circumstances, to
give a great deal of attention to one of many remarkable promises made to her by our Lord—to one of
many of the practices of devotion to His Sacred
Heart taught her by Him.

(ii) The whole devotion to the Sacred Heart was
only very gradually and in the most guarded and
unobtrusive way made known by the Saint. For
about eleven or twelve years it was not revealed

---

[1] In a letter to Fr. Herbert Thurston, S.J., quoted by him in
The Month, 1903, p. 642. Cf. also Hamon, *Histoire*, IV, 55, note 2.

even to the members of her own monastery. Even in the later years of her life it was taught only with much reserve and chiefly in documents which were not made public for a long time after her death. The circumstances of the time demanded this great caution in reference to a devotion whose form was new and much misunderstood, and whose propagation was to arouse violent opposition. If her reticence about the ' Great Promise ' argues that she was doubtful about it, or indifferent to its importance, then we can fairly argue that—in due proportion—she was doubtful about and indifferent to the great revelations that she had received and the entire devotion to the Sacred Heart. This was certainly not the case.

Objection III. Until about 1870 (when, apparently, leaflets containing the text of the ' Great Promise ' were widely disseminated)[1] little or nothing was heard of the Promise ; and even since that date books and leaflets have been published which omit the ' Great ' or ' Twelfth ' Promise, in the list of the promises made to St. Margaret Mary by our Lord. All this suggests, at least, that the authenticity of the Promise is suspect.

Reply. (i) The text of the ' Great Promise ' *is* found in several MSS. of undeniable authenticity, and though the autograph of the letter on which the versions of the text in these MSS. are based is not extant, there is excellent evidence that they give us a faithful reproduction of the original. No valid argument has, in fact, been brought forward against the historical authenticity of the existing texts.

(ii) The Promise *was* known shortly after the death of St. Margaret Mary to the Visitation Community at Paray (as its inclusion in the ' Life ' by the *Contemporaines* shows), to the Community at Moulins

---

[1] Cf. Le Bachelet, *Études,* 1901 (Vol. 88), p. 386 ; Thurston, *The Month,* 1903, p. 636.

(which began the Nine Fridays in 1714),[1] to Mgr. Languet, one of the first biographers of the Saint,[2] to Gabriel Nicollet, who in his book *Le Parfait Adorateur du Sacré-Cœur de Jésus*, published in 1761, quotes from Mgr. Languet on the Promise.[3]

(iii) The actual text of the 'Great Promise' was not published until 1867, when the Monastery of Paray issued the first edition of *Vie et Œuvres*. Only then did the original text of the letter to Mother de Saumaise and the 'Life' by the *Contemporaines*, become available to the public. Before that date only the modified account of the Promise which Archbishop Languet had given in his Life of the Saint, had been published. Following the beatification of St. Margaret Mary in 1864 and the publication of *Vie et Œuvres*, 1867, came a renewal of interest in the Saint, the 'Great Promise' became popularly known, and the practice of the 'Nine Fridays' spread rapidly.

(iv) The silence concerning the 'Great Promise' of early writers (such as Croiset and Galliffet) on St. Margaret Mary, or on the devotion to the Sacred Heart, is due to the fact that either they did not know of the Promise, or if they did, they were afraid to publish it, and this for very good reasons. Only by very slow stages after the death of the Saint did the devotion to the Sacred Heart, as revealed to her, become known. In the testimonies of her contemporaries at the diocesan process of 1715,[4] in the *Circulaire* of Paray sent (1691) to the different monasteries of the Visitation after her death,[5] and giving an account of her life, there is very little said about the devotion. Jansenism was at its height in France, and it opposed the new devotion by every means, fair and foul. The greatest outcry was raised

---

[1] *Circulaire de Moulins* (*V.O.*, III, 477).
[2] *La Vie*, etc., 1729, Bk. VII, p. 241.
[3] p. 112. [4] *V.O.*, I, 441 *sqq.* [5] *V.O.*, I, 571 *sqq.*

against it. Every pretext was seized upon to belittle and throw doubt on the revelations of Margaret Mary[1]—then but a simple and unknown religious. The Church itself did not at first by any means encourage the devotion, and it was only painfully and slowly in the teeth of fierce opposition that it won its way to official recognition. The friends of the devotion to the Sacred Heart from the days of the Saint of Paray had a very hard task in having the devotion properly understood and in winning for it the approbation of the Church. It was most natural that in such circumstances one particular act of the devotion—the Nine First Fridays—should be overlooked or, more probably, not emphasized. Even to this day the authenticity and still more the interpretation of the ' Great Promise ' raise difficulties, how much more so at a time when the entire devotion to the Sacred Heart was a subject of acrid dispute and when it and its great apostle, St. Margaret Mary, had not yet received the recognition and approbation of the Church. Only in the first part of the eighteenth century did the cause of the Saint of Paray come up for the official examination, and only in 1864 was she beatified and her sanctity confirmed and her mission (now so fully recognized) realized.

The ' Great Promise ' is such a remarkable one—such a marvel of Divine mercy—that many of those who have given it consideration, either before 1867 (when it was possible for it to be known only to the few), or since, have concluded—if their knowledge was not extensive—that there *must* be something ' fishy ' about it, it must be a ' holy ' exaggeration which, probably, had no real historical foundation, and must, at best, be put in the category of a ' pious belief.' Others more learned, have not studied the

[1] Cf. Decree de ' Tuto ' (1918) for the canonization of the Saint (*V.O.*, III, 169 *sqq.*).

E

historical basis of the Promise, but have seen in it obvious theological difficulties, and have concluded that it *cannot* be authentic, or, if it is, its interpretation must be such that it means little or nothing and is, therefore, unworthy of serious attention. Others, again, have been startled by the consequences of accepting the Promise as it stands, and have been moved to reject its authenticity (or at least any reasonable interpretation of it) because of the abuses to which, they consider, it is open. For these reasons (all of which will be dealt with in the course of this book) it is not a matter of wonder that the Promise was not well known before the publication of St. Margaret Mary's writings, and since has been neglected or treated with suspicion or even frowned upon in certain quarters.

It may be, too, that just as the entire devotion to the Sacred Heart as taught to St. Margaret Mary by our Divine Lord was, in the designs of Providence, only slowly and by very gradual stages to be made known to the world, so it was the divine will that only in our own day—when the great mercy which the Promise announces seems most needed—should the devotion of the Nine First Fridays be widely known and appreciated and practised.

Among writers who have seriously studied the historical authenticity of the ' Great Promise,' there is almost unanimity in accepting it as certainly genuine. From the beginning the *Contemporaines* and Archbishop Languet accepted its authenticity. Of modern writers, Archbishop Gauthey, in his critical editions (1915 and 1920) of the Life and Works of St. Margaret Mary, accepts the Promise, and so do Frs. Bainvel, du Bovays de la Begassière, Estébanez, Galeazzi, Hamon, Hättenschwiller, Le Bachelet, McDonnell, Masella, Nix, Vermeersch and Canon Truptin in the books or articles which are mentioned in the bibliography (p. xv).[1] Thus Père Hamon writes, ' On peut affirmer en toute rigueur historique que les théologiens ont le droit de tirer du texte de la lettre de 1688 tout ce que leur science leur permettra d'en tirer, à la plus grande consolation des âmes chrétiennes, et à la plus grande gloire du Sacré-Cœur de Jésus. Il a pour nous la valeur d'un autographe.'[2] Canon Truptin says, ' Cette lettre [of St. Margaret Mary to Mother de Saumaise] est d'une authenticité certaine.'[3] Fr. Vermeersch: 'Le doute n'est donc pas possible, pour tout ce qui est essentiel dans la Promesse, nous possédons un témoinage authentique de la Sainte.'[4] Fr. Estébanez: ' La Grande Promesse . . . a une valeur historique indisputable,'[5] and ' La Grande Promesse est si certaine et si authentique, historiquement parlant, qu'on ne peut rien exiger de plus.'[6] Fr. H. Ramière in the *Messager du Sacré-Cœur* (1883) and Fr. Terrien in *La Dévotion au Sacré-Cœur de Jésus* (1902, Appendix IV), also defend the authenticity of the ' Great Promise ' ; and even that very cautious savant, Fr. Herbert Thurston, finds no sufficient reason for doubting the authenticity of the letter. ' The autograph is no longer in existence,' he writes,[7] ' but none the less from the contemporaneous character of the extant copies and from other considerations which I hope to develop in *The Month*,[8] the evidence in favour of its genuineness must be regarded, I think, as conclusive.' And subsequently, to his article in *The Month*, he wrote :[9] ' Speaking historically, the evidence for the authenticity of the

---

[1] Fr. Estébanez (pp. 40 and 73 *sqq.*) gives as champions of the authenticity of the ' Great Promise ' these writers also : Fathers Bengœchea, Boudinhon, Boubée, Coubée, Guillaume, Lejeune, Redon, Smit and Suau. [2] *Études*, 1903 (Vol. 95), p. 857.
[3] p. 20. [4] II, p. 132. [5] p. 2. [6] p. 19.
[7] *The Tablet*, 1903 (Vol. LXIX), p. 777.
[8] Cf. *The Month*, 1903, pp. 635-649. [9] *The Tablet*, 1903, p. 977.

letter to the Mère de Saumaise seems to be precise and trustworthy.'

Alone among the writers whose works I have been able to consult, Fr. Joseph J. C. Petrovits, in his book entitled *Devotion to the Sacred Heart* (which was published in the United States of America in 1918), attempts to make out a case,[1] both on historical and theological grounds against the authenticity of the 'Great Promise.' Having argued at length he reaches this somewhat unexpected conclusion : ' From the perusal of the accessible evidence it seems fairly certain that Blessed Margaret Mary actually wrote a letter in which she advocated a devotion similar to the present devotion of the Nine Fridays ' (p. 238). Later on in his book, Fr. Petrovits proceeds to argue in favour of a certain interpretation of the Promise which, after all, suggests that he does not really believe that it is spurious. The case which Fr. Petrovits makes out against the authenticity of the Promise is, in my opinion, anything but a strong one, and his chief arguments are considered and answered (satisfactorily, I hope) in the present volume.

It is interesting to note that the ' Great Promise ' —alone of all the promises which our Lord made to St. Margaret Mary in favour of those who practise or propagate devotion to His Sacred Heart—is embodied in the bull of canonization *Ecclesiæ Consuetudo antiquissima*[2] of the Saint (1920). While this inclusion does not commit the Church to an official confirmation of the historical authenticity of the Promise,[3] it does, surely, at least, imply that the Church has no good reason for believing the Promise to be spurious.[4]

---

[1] pp. 166 *sqq.*   [2] *Acta Apostolicæ Sedis*, 1920, p. 503.

[3] See *infra*, pp. 53 and 55.

[4] Fr. Vermeersch goes further. He writes ' D'ailleurs, toute insistance est maintenant superflue, puisque le texte de la Grande Promesse a été intégralement inseré dans la Bulle de canonisation de Sainte Marguerite-Marie ' (p. 137).

CHAPTER VI

In the preceding chapter the evidence for the historical authenticity of the ' Great Promise ' was examined,
and it was shown that there is quite satisfactory proof
that the Promise is found in the authentic writings of
St. Margaret Mary and that its text has come down to
us substantially intact.   Now it is necessary to
inquire into the theological soundness of the Promise,
i.e. have we sufficient evidence for prudently believing
that the Promise is of divine origin—was really made
to the Saint by our Lord ? The ' Great Promise ' is
one of may private revelations made to St. Margaret
Mary, and so we must consider the question of private
revelations and the attitude of the Church to them.

A. *Private Revelations :*

To reveal is to unveil—to make known something
that was previously hidden.   Divine revelation is the
supernatural unfolding—directly or indirectly—of
some truth by God to men, it is divine testimony,
divine guarantee of the truth of something.   When
God reveals we have absolute certainty of truth,
since He can neither deceive nor be deceived, and so
we accept and assent to such a truth with what is
termed ' divine faith.'   In the dispensation under
which we live God has made known to us, through
His Son and the Paraclete whom He sent, a certain
body of truths called the ' deposit of faith.'   These

truths were entrusted to the Apostles, and through them to the Church, and were given for the acceptance of all mankind, and are binding on the assent of all. They make up what is called 'public revelation.' This revelation came to an end with the death of the last of the Apostles (St. John). God will add no more to it, and the Church cannot do so, for public revelation—the 'deposit of faith '—is committed to her not to add to it, but to preserve it intact, to hand it on complete and unchanged, to certify its divine origin, and to expound and interpret it with infallible authority.

Private revelation, on the other hand, is the divine unfolding of truth, in a supernatural way, whenever God so wills, to an individual for his benefit or for the benefit of others. Such an unveiling of truth may consist in the explanation of a truth which had been already revealed, or the making known of an entirely new truth. While a private revelation must be accepted and with divine faith (granted that the recipient of the revelation has satisfactory evidence of its divine origin) by the person to whom it is made, and by those to whom it may be directed by God, it is not binding on the acceptance and belief of all the faithful ; it is not even intended, in many cases, for the instruction of the Church at large,[1] though the entire Church may indirectly benefit by it. Such a revelation cannot, and does not, become part of the 'deposit of faith,' is not directly committed to the guardianship of the Church, is not accompanied (as public revelation is) by any divine guarantee that it will be transmitted unchanged to others, and can never become the object of an act of 'Catholic faith.'[2]

[1] The revelations of St. Margaret Mary were so intended.

[2] 'Divine faith ' means the acceptance of a truth because God has revealed it ; ' Catholic faith ' the acceptance of a truth because God has revealed it, and the Church proposes it for acceptance as part of the 'deposit of faith.'

Private revelation is used not to teach a new doctrine of the faith, but to guide human conduct.[1]

A private revelation is ordinarily made to any individual either by (A) a vision, or (B) by supernatural speech.

(A) A *vision* is the supernatural perception of an object which could not be perceived by man in a natural way. It may be (i) *a bodily*, or *sensible vision*—called an 'apparition'—when something which would naturally be invisible is seen with the bodily eye (either because some external figure—present either in substance or present only in appearance which consists in a certain arrangement of luminous rays—is really present and affects the eye in the ordinary way or because an agent superior to man directly modifies the visual organ and produces in the composite a sensation equivalent to that which an external object would produce), such were many of the apparitions of our Lord after the Ascension, e.g., in the Blessed Eucharist, and the apparitions of our Blessed Lady at Lourdes ; (ii) an *imaginative vision*, produced in the imagination (i.e. the sensible representation of an object by the action of the imagination alone, without the aid of the bodily eye), a kind of vision which generally occurs in sleep, e.g. the visions of the angel to St. Joseph; (iii) an *intellectual vision*, in which the mind perceives a truth without any sensible image, e.g. St. Teresa's vision of the Blessed Trinity. A bodily or an imaginative vision may be accompanied by an intellectual vision explaining its meaning ; all three kinds of vision may occur together, e.g. St. Paul's vision on the road to Damascus was sensible when he perceived ' a light from heaven shining round about him ' (Acts ix, 3), it was imaginative when, still corporally blind, he saw Ananias

---

[1] Cf. S. Thomas, *Summa*, IIa, IIæ, Q. CLXXIV, Art. 6, *ad* 3.

' coming in and putting his hands upon him ' (Acts ix, 12), and intellectual when he understood God's will in his regard.

(B) Another way in which a divine revelation is made to an individual is by *supernatural speech*, i.e. by words produced in a supernatural way and which are heard either externally, by the ear, as in ordinary speech, or internally, in the imagination, or which are addressed directly to the intellect itself.

When a truth is made known by God to an individual, either by vision or by supernatural speech, or in any other way, the recipient grasps the truth with entire clearness and with complete assurance of its veracity.   If, however, he must convey it to others, there is a *possibility* of error arising, not in regard to the substance of the truth, but in reference to details, for the divine thought must now be clothed in human language.   The possibility of error in detail will arise from the fact that (a) it is difficult, if not impossible, to convey in limited human language the most sublime divine thoughts, and the human recipient of divine revelation may fail to convey clearly and completely the divine mind, and (b) in endeavouring to do so he may unconsciously add to or detract from the divine revelation, or consciously endeavour to explain or interpret it, and so introduce some detail which was not given in the original revelation (this is evident from the examination of such private revelations as those of St. Gertrude).

Human instruments of divine operations and human language have their necessary natural limitations, and in employing secondary causes, God uses them according to their nature.   Substantial error in translating the revelation into human language will be avoided not only by the sincere desire of the recipient to convey the exact truth, but still more by the Providence of God watching over the transmission of His revelation. God will, doubtless, see that the essential truth is conveyed unchanged, but He will not prevent the defects in detail that may arise in the natural process of passing the revelation through the conduit of the human mind to express it in words. That this is so is clear from the critical examination of the private revelations of many of the great mystics, e.g. of those of St. Teresa. Hence it is that all private revelations, even the most authoritative, the most evidently divine, need to be carefully studied and critically examined by experts, that the exact truth may be reached by the application of sane criticism.

The truth of private revelations is tested by scientific examination of (a) the character (natural, ascetical, mystical) of the recipient, (b) the manner and the circumstances in which the revelation was received, (c) the content of the revelation, (d) its effects.

The authenticity of private revelations is entirely a *historical question*—a matter of human evidence. It is no part of the Church's business to guarantee such authenticity, and she does not do so. Even were the Church entirely satisfied—on historical grounds—as to the authenticity of a private revelation, she does not and cannot add its content to the ' deposit of faith,' or propose it for the acceptance of all the faithful, nor is the infallibility of her teaching authority in any way involved in dealing with private revelations. Ordinarily she does not concern herself with them at all, except to keep a watchful eye on them to see that they do not lead the faithful into error in belief or practice. Their authenticity is entirely a question for historical investigation and proof as is any other event of human history ; their content a matter for private individuals to pass judgment on and—apart from the actual recipients of the revelation—to accept

or reject as they think fit.[1] When private revelations
were made to a person that the Church beatifies, then
they are subject to a rigorous examination and criticism
and the Church approves them in a *negative* way,
i.e. to this extent that she carefully examines the
writings of the recipient and declares them free of
anything ' that merits theological censure,' and she
rigorously investigates the life of the recipient and
pronounces authoritatively that he (she) practised
virtue in a heroic degree, and that miracles have been
worked in confirmation of his (her) sanctity. If the
Church, on occasion, goes further and gives a certain
amount of positive approbation to certain private
revelations (as those of St. Hildegard approved in
part by Eugene III, of St. Bridget of Sweden by
Boniface IX, of St. Catherine of Siena by Gregory
XVI), all that the approbation means—as Benedict
XIV explains—is ' permission after mature examination to publish these revelations for the instruction
and benefit of the faithful, for though the assent of
Catholic faith is neither due, nor can be given, to
these revelations, even when so approved, they should
be believed with a human assent according to the rules
of prudence which show them to be probable and
piously worthy of credence.'[2] And Pius X, in his
Encyclical, *Pascendi,* against modernism (1907), having
recalled that ecclesiastical authority does not permit
private revelations to be published except with great
precautions, adds that even then the Church does not
guarantee the truth of the fact of revelation, but
simply does not stand in the way of giving credence
to things for which motives of human belief are not

[1] Some revelations (like the ' Great Promise ') are subjected to
the most searching investigation and the most critical study because
of their practical importance and the interest that they arouse.

[2] Benedict XIV, *De Canonizatione Sanctorum* (1743), Bk. II,
c. 32, *n.* 11.

wanting. The Congregation of Sacred Rites, having been questioned about the apparitions and revelations of Lourdes and La Salette, replied that ' such apparitions and revelations had been neither approved nor condemned by the Apostolic See, but merely permitted as piously to be accepted solely by human faith, according to the tradition in their favour confirmed by proper evidence.'[1] Hence the Church's approval of private revelations is very limited. It does not imply that the Church—even when she submits them to careful examination, and is satisfied about their historical authenticity—in any way guarantees this authenticity or the truth or accuracy of their content. All that is a matter for human investigation and proof as in the case of any other alleged fact of human history.[2] When there is satisfactory historical proof for the authenticity of a private revelation it may be accepted and acted upon—indeed, even the Church herself accepts in practice certain private revelations (this is the case with the revelations of St. Margaret Mary)[3] as historically true and acts upon them.[4]

[1] S.R.C. 3419[2] (1877).

[2] Hence the Church will not (as the simple faithful sometimes think she ought) give any formal—much less infallible—decision regarding the authenticity of the ' Great Promise.' Such a question does not fall within her province.

[3] See below, pp. 59 *sqq.*

[4] 'Nor can the Church' (writes Rev. P. Finlay, S.J., in *Divine Faith*, 1917, p. 58), ' by her approval, alter in any way the character of a private revelation; she cannot insert it in the " deposit of faith "; she cannot even declare that it may be inferred from that "deposit." Indeed, her gift of infallibility does not extend to deciding on the authenticity of private revelations at all. No doubt she may judge, and often judge infallibly, of their doctrinal truth and meaning. But as their authenticity is entirely distinct from the doctrines they may involve, and was neither revealed to the Apostles nor to be inferred from any of the things revealed to them, it lies wholly without the domain of infallible Church decisions. And, indeed, the Church has never made either claim or attempt to decide the authenticity of any private revelation. She often inquires into such revelations in her processes of beatification and canonization, examining

B. *The Revelations of St. Margaret Mary :*

Whether St. Margaret Mary received revelations from our Divine Lord, and whether she recorded them correctly and transmitted them faithfully is a matter of evidence—a question of history, not of faith. Authentic private revelations are invariably made only to persons of high sanctity—persons raised to the mystic state—and often by means of visions accompanied by words, as in the case of St. Margaret Mary. Ordinarily, we have to depend on the recipient for an account of them, for usually they are confined to that person alone. Accordingly, we must investigate the following questions in the case of the revelations of the Saint of Paray (with which alone we are concerned) : (i) Is she a truthful and trustworthy witness who does not deliberately deceive us ? (ii) What evidence is there that she herself was not deceived—the subject of error or illusion in regard to her revelations ?

The first question is sufficiently answered by the fact that the Church has canonized the Saint, and before doing so, made a thorough investigation of her writings and of the practice of virtue in a heroic degree in her life, and had adequate proof of the performance of miracles (five in all) in testimony of the power of her intercession in heaven. All that is sufficient evidence, even on merely historical grounds, for the trustworthiness of St. Margaret Mary. Her canonization does not, however, guarantee that she may not have been in error or the victim of delusions in reference to her revelations.

if they contain anything opposed to the settled doctrine of the Church or to generally received Catholic teaching. And she sometimes gives them a very qualified approval, usually to particular revelations, rarely—if ever—to a saint's revelations as a whole. But such approval, even if given, has a very limited significance. It does not imply that the Church in any way guarantees the authenticity of the revelations or the truth and accuracy of their contents.'

To determine whether Margaret Mary Alacoque—on whose own evidence we have to depend for the fact of her revelations—was likely to have been led into error or the subject of illusion, it is necessary to examine her character (natural, ascetical and mystical), the content of her revelations and their effects. Regarding her character we have the evidence of her writings—which are ' master-pieces of good sense, cleverness and judgment '[1]—and the extrinsic testimony of her superiors (Mothers de Saumaise and Greyfié who tested her severely in her religious life) ; of her spiritual directors, the Blessed Claude de la Colombière, S.J. (noted in his day as a most wise and prudent director with a remarkable gift of ' discernment of spirits'), and Fr. Rolin, S.J. ; of her contemporaries in religion (many of whom lived in daily contact with her for years, and thirty-one of whom gave sworn testimony about her life at the informative process for her beatification in 1715), and of her secular contemporaries, her relatives, friends and correspondents. From these we learn that Margaret Mary was naturally simple, calm, straightforward, prudent, and endowed with great common sense.[2] Though not well educated, she was intelligent, and while not imaginative, she was impressionable and of delicate feeling. In her religious life she gave ample proof of solid and tried virtue. She was especially noted for her deep humility[3] (far from desiring notoriety in regard to her wonderful relations with our

---

[1] Père Hamon in *Études*, 1904 (Vol. 100), p. 27.

[2] She held in her community the important offices of Assistant and Mistress of Novices and would have been appointed Superior had she not begged our Lord to intervene and prevent this. She was often consulted by outsiders—ecclesiastical and lay—on important matters, so great was her reputation for wisdom, prudence and good sense.

[3] Speaking of her great humility, her low opinion of herself and her desire to be despised and remain unknown, Archbishop Gauthey writes (*V.O.*, I, 17) : ' It is precisely this attitude of Margaret Mary

Lord she kept everything secret, save from her superiors and directors, and only towards the end of her life was the veil slightly lifted when she was obliged by our Lord's command to begin the promotion of the devotion to His Sacred Heart ; over and over again she begged that her writings should be burned), for a most exact obedience in all things, and especially in all that concerned her revelations ; for a great love of obscurity and of suffering, of which our Lord made her the almost constant victim. She distrusted herself, being well aware of the possibility of error or illusion in reference to her revelations and her mission. To the end of her life she was troubled— and often in her writings expressed her fear and distress—lest she should be deceived or deceive others, but she was reassured both by the special signs given and the wonders worked by our Lord in testimony of the reality of her revelations, and by her spiritual directors and superiors.[1] These natural qualities of intelligence and common sense, these supernatural virtues of humility, obedience and distrust of self furnish the best guarantee against the possibility of error or hallucination on the part of St. Margaret Mary in reference to her revelations.

It is not necessary to treat here at any length of the content of the Saint's revelations and the effects which they produced. The devotion to the Sacred Heart which Margaret Mary taught and promoted is now so widely known and well established, and its effects are so patent and wonderful, that no one any longer questions the truth, orthodoxy, or fruitfulness of her revelations.

which gives evidence, in face of the most exacting criticism, of the truth of the revelations which were made to her and which she has communicated to men on God's behalf.'

[1] Detailed references are not given for these statements. They can be verified by consulting *V.O.*, *passim*, or any standard Life of the Saint, e.g. Father Hamon's.

C. *The Church and the Revelations of St. Margaret Mary* :

In canonizing St. Margaret Mary the Church has given us an assurance that her writings contain nothing that merits theological censure,[1] and that she practised virtue in a heroic degree.[2] Furthermore, in a twofold way, the Church has recognized that the visions and revelations of the Saint, taken as a whole, rest on a satisfactory historical basis and that she accepts their content in substance :

(*a*) The Church in many official documents refers to the visions and revelations, and obviously accepts their truth as an ordinary historical fact, based on sound human evidence which is worthy of credence. This she does not only in the Brief of beatification (1864) and the Bull of canonization (1920) of St. Margaret Mary, and in the liturgical formulas of the Mass and the Divine Office for the feasts of the Sacred Heart, and of St. Margaret Mary (October 17), but also in important official pronouncements, e.g. the Constitution, *Benignæ* (June 28, 1889), and the Encyclical, *Annum Sacrum* (May 25, 1899), of Leo XIII on devotion to the Sacred Heart, the letter of the Congregation of Sacred Rites to the bishops of the world on the same subject,[3] the Encyclical, *Miserentissimus Redemptor* (May 8, 1928), of Pius XI on the Common Reparation due to the Most Sacred Heart of Jesus.

(*b*) While the devotion to the Sacred Heart is, in its theological foundations (the doctrines of the Incarnation, of the love of God for men, of His desire for their salvation, etc.), quite independent of the revelations of St. Margaret Mary, and while it is partly independent even in its historical foundation (in so far as

---

[1] Decree of the Congregation of S. Rites, September 22, 1827.
[2] S.R.C., August 23, 1846.   [3] July 21, 1899 (S.R.C. 4045).

devotion to the Sacred Heart, in one form or another, was known to and practised by a limited number of elect souls even from the eleventh century),[1] yet it is indisputable, as a matter of historical fact, that the devotion, in the form in which it has been officially received and approved by the Church and is now practised throughout the entire Catholic body, has a most intimate historical connection with and has, indeed, sprung from the visions and revelations of the Saint of Paray-le-Monial.[2]   It is from these that (i) a clear knowledge of the precise nature of *the formal object* of the devotion—the physical Heart of Christ, living and united hypostatically with the Divine Person of the Word, regarded as the symbol of His love for God, His Father, and of His love for men, a love despised, forgotten and outraged—and of the exact *end* of the devotion (a love of reparation given by men to Christ) has been derived ;   (ii) the chief practices[3] of the devotion to the Sacred Heart embodying the desires of Christ for a love of reparation—i.e. acts of consecration and atonement, the Holy Hour, the Communion of reparation on the First Friday of the month—have sprung.

To these visions and revelations of St. Margaret Mary we owe the establishment by the Church of the feast of the Sacred Heart (with definite practices attached to it) on the Friday following the octave of Corpus Christi and the selection of the First Friday of the month as a day of special atonement ; to them we are indebted for the authentic and recognized image of the Divine Heart (a heart on

[1] Cf. pp. 16 *sqq.*

[2] Cf. Brief of Leo XIII (1890), (*V.O.*, III, 226) ; Decree of S.R.C. on miracles for the canonization of St. Margaret Mary (1918) (*V.O.*,III, 160) ; Benedict XV to Abp. Gauthey (1916) (*V.O.*, I, 2) ; Bainvel, pp. 103–4 ; *Dictionnaire de Théologie*, III, 293; J. Bricout in *Ecclesia* (1928), p. 206 ; Nix., p. 79.

[3] Cf. Encyclical, *Miserentissimus Redemptor* (1928).

fire and radiant, wounded, girt with thorns and sur-
mounted by a cross) and an understanding of its meaning and the practice of honouring it ;[1] to them we owe
the Promises made by Christ in favour of those who
practise and promote devotion to His Adorable Heart.

From all this it is clear that the Church has in a
very special way recognized that the revelations of
St. Margaret Mary are, in general, historically and
theologically, acceptable.[2] This does *not* mean,
however, that the Church *guarantees* their authenticity—this is no part of her duty, as was already
explained—it is a matter of ordinary historical
evidence, not a question of faith ;[3] nor does it mean
that, while accepting their historical authenticity on
ordinary historical grounds, and their theological
orthodoxy *taken as a whole*, the Church stands
sponsor for any particular revelation among them.

D. *The ' Great Promise ' :*

In support of the theological soundness of the
' Great Promise,' i.e. in favour of the view that the
Promise is what it claims to be, a genuine revelation
made to St. Margaret Mary by our Divine Lord and,
therefore, of divine origin, the following arguments
are offered :

(1) There is excellent reason, historical and theological, for believing the revelations of the Saint to be
genuine and worthy of acceptance by prudent minds.
Among these revelations is the ' Great Promise.'[4] If
other revelations of St. Margaret Mary and other
promises of the Sacred Heart to her be accepted as
genuine, and they are, then the ' Great Promise '

---

[1] It was for honouring the image of the Sacred Heart that the
first Promises of our Lord to St. Margaret Mary were made.

[2] Cf. Bainvel, p. 103 ; *Dictionnaire de Théologie*, III, 293.

[3] In the Church's recognition of the visions and revelations of
St. Margaret Mary not her infallibility is at stake, but her reputation
for sound scholarship and for prudent and authoritative judgement
(cf. Bainvel, p. 103).   [4] See Chapter V.

F

should also be accepted unless good reasons be given for doubting its genuineness. The presumption is in its favour and those who call in question its authenticity—either historical or theological—should give good reasons for their doubts and suspicions (which mainly arise either from want of knowledge or from *a priori* reasoning about the content of the Promise).

(2) The very clear and precise terms of the 'Great Promise' make it impossible to believe that St. Margaret Mary could have been in error about it or that it could be the result of an illusion. It is not a vague general statement on an abstract question, but concerns a very definite and concrete practice about which the Saint cannot have had any preconceived ideas. It embodies, too, a practice that is in entire conformity with the general devotion to the Sacred Heart—great mercy to sinners, Communion of reparation on the First Friday of the month, special succour at the hour of death for those who honoured the Sacred Heart, all these are leading features of devotion to the Divine Heart as it was revealed to St. Margaret Mary.

(3) Examination of the accounts given by the recipients of private revelations has sometimes shown that there is room for error and a possibility of alteration when they have endeavoured to explain or interpret the revelations. In the case of the 'Great Promise,' St. Margaret Mary does not attempt any explanation or suggest any interpretation of the Promise. She states quite simply : 'One Friday, during Holy Communion, He said these words to His unworthy servant, if she is not mistaken, "I promise thee," ' etc.[1]

---

[1] *V.O.* (Letter 86), II, p. 397. It is interesting to remark that the Saint was forbidden to read over and correct what she wrote about her revelations. This was (remarks Père Boubée, in *Études*, 1916, p. 747) to prevent the possibility of her mixing her personal reflections and her conscious ego with the inspirations of Grace.

(4) While the Church does not and cannot guarantee the authenticity of the ' Great Promise ' (this, as we have many times remarked, is a matter of historical evidence), and while she has given no official interpretation of it (and is never likely to do so), it is noteworthy that :

(a) The Promise was carefully examined in Rome at the time of the examination of the writings of St. Margaret Mary (1827), and when her life was being investigated (1846) in view of her beatification. In the copy of the letter to Mother de Saumaise, containing the Promise which was sent to Rome for examination by the Congregation of Sacred Rites, the Promise was heavily underlined to prevent it being overlooked.[1] That it was not overlooked is shown by the discussion on it that took place between the Promotor Fidei and the Postulator of the Cause.[2] Nothing in it was found worthy of censure.

(b) In the Bull of Canonization of St. Margaret Mary (1920) the ' Great Promise ' is included, and in the long account of the Saint's life which is given in the Bull, it is the only one of the Promises which finds mention. We cannot conclude from this that the Church officially guarantees the authenticity of the Promise, but we can reasonably conclude from its inclusion in the carefully prepared official document of canonization that the Church is, at least, satisfied that there is no good reason—on either historical or theological grounds—for rejecting the Promise as spurious or unsound.[3] It must be susceptible, too, of a perfectly orthodox interpretation.

[1] Cf. Vermeersch, p. 136, note 1 ; Thurston, p. 637 ; Galeazzi, p. 145 ; Hamon, I, 434, note 3.   [2] See below, p. 96.
[3] Fr. Vermeersch (who alone of the authors mentioned on p. 46 has written on the authenticity of the Promise since 1920) writes : ' Besides all insistence [on its authenticity] is now superfluous, since the text of the " Great Promise " has been inserted in full in the Bull of canonization of St. Margaret Mary ' (p. 137).

(c) Since 1867 when the writings of St. Margaret Mary were collected and published in full for the first time, and the Promise was, therefore, brought into the light of day, the devotion of the Nine First Fridays has spread and grown steadily throughout the Catholic world and has taken firm root among the people in most, if not in all countries.[1] This has happened under the watchful eye of the bishops and of Rome itself. In every country priests in the pulpit, in the schools and in the confessional, have taught and encouraged the devotion. Many of the bishops have favoured it. A multitude of books and leaflets about it have been written and widely disseminated. Some of the greatest theologians of our day (e.g. Fr. Vermeersch, S.J.) have not hesitated to defend and explain the Promise and give it a wide and generous interpretation ; while leading historians of the devotion to the Sacred Heart (e.g. Frs. Hamon, S.J., Bainvel, S.J.) have investigated and fully accepted the ' Great Promise.'

E. *Conclusion :*

When considering the question of the historical authenticity of the ' Great Promise ' (in Chapter V), we argued that there is ample evidence to show that the text of the Promise was given in a letter written by St. Margaret Mary to her former Superior,

---

[1] By personal investigation (mainly through a questionnaire addressed to the directors of the Apostleship of Prayer throughout the world), I have learned that the devotion of the Nine Fridays is known, and in nearly every case is extensively and enthusiastically practised in the following countries : (a) *Europe*—Austria, Belgium, Czechoslovakia, Denmark, France, Germany, Great Britain, Holland, Hungary, Italy, Ireland, Jugoslavia, Malta, Poland, Portugal, Spain and Switzerland ; (b) *America*—Argentine, Canada, Ecuador, Nicaragua, United States, Uruguay, Venezuela ; (c) *Asia*—China, Japan, Palestine, Syria : (d) *Africa*—Egypt, Madagascar, Togo and (e) in *Australia*. My queries did not receive a reply from : Albania, Belgian Congo, Brazil, Ceylon, Colombia, Cuba, Finland, Greece, India, Mexico, Paraguay, Rumania, Salvador.

Mother de Saumaise, and that it has been transmitted to us—in several MS. copies—unchanged. Was the Saint in error or the subject of an illusion when she wrote so directly and so simply the words, ' One Friday, during Holy Communion, He said these words to His unworthy servant, if she is not mistaken, " I promise thee," ' etc. ? That is the question of the theological soundness of the Promise. In this chapter we have given evidence in a very brief form (based on the character, natural and ascetical, of St. Margaret Mary and on the content and effects of her revelations) that the Saint's revelations as a whole are undoubtedly genuine and that there is no valid reason—historical or theological[1]—for believing that the ' Great Promise ' is any different from her other revelations. That while the Church does not and cannot guarantee the authenticity of the Promise she has given it a certain measure of approval (might we not claim that she has given it the greatest measure of approval that is possible ?) not merely in a negative way, but also positively, both indirectly—by her acceptance of the historical truth of St. Margaret Mary's revelations in general and of her mission from Christ to teach and promote devotion to His Sacred Heart and to encourage and propagate it by His promises of signal favours—and directly, by her attitude to the ' Great Promise ' in practice. We may, therefore, claim for the authenticity of the Promise the certainty known as *moral certitude*— that kind of certainty which alone is or can be given to matters of historical fact—namely that, while the authenticity of the Promise is not self-evident, nor is it proved so conclusively that there is no possibility of doubt concerning its genuineness, there is such ample and satisfactory evidence in its favour, coupled

[1] The apparent theological objections to the Promise are considered in Chapter VIII (pp. 98 *sqq.*).

with the fact that no evidence of any real weight has been adduced against it,[1] *we may accept its authenticity as beyond reasonable and prudent doubt.*

That this is the considered opinion of authors of eminence and authority who have written at length on the ' Great Promise ' is shown by the following brief citations, which could be multiplied at will. (*a*) Fr. Vermeersch writes[2]—' The Promise has claims to be admitted by us, not as an incontestable truth, but as one of those facts morally proved, which the mind accepts without anxiety and without any positive doubt ' ; (*b*) Fr. Galeazzi : ' The Promise is then furnished with all the conditions which are necessary that it be admitted, not, indeed, as a fact absolutely and metaphysically certain, but as one of those facts morally investigated and proved and so *morally certain*, the authenticity and authority of which may be a.lmitted without anxiety and *without any positive doubt* ' ;[3]   (*c*) Fr. Estébanez : ' the revelation of this Promise is certain, *humanly speaking* ; in sane criticism this cannot be denied ' ;[4] (*d*) Fr. Bainvel : ' The Saint's assertion [in the Great Promise '] is no more absolute here than elsewhere.   But having regard to the sincerity of the witness it affords a guarantee of the true mind of a saintly soul.   And as we have solid reasons for believing in the Saint's supernatural mission, these same reasons hold good for the reality of the Promise.'[5]

[1] See p. 48.   [2] II, 137.   [3] p. 40.
[4] p. 59.   [5] p. 57, note 3.

CHAPTER VII

THE ' Great Promise ' was made known by St. Margaret Mary in a letter[1] which she wrote, between 1687 and 1689, to Mother de Saumaise then at Dijon. This saintly religious had been Margaret Mary's superior at Paray from 1672 to 1678, that is during the years of the ' great ' apparitions and revelations of the Sacred Heart ; she was the Saint's first and greatest confidante, and to her Margaret Mary (as she explains in letters to Mother de Saumaise) opened her heart as to no one else ; she, too, was chosen by Christ (as He told the Saint more than once) to be one of the first promoters of devotion to His Sacred Heart and destined for great rewards from Him. In the course of this letter, in which she speaks of the Sacred Heart and of His great mercies, she writes :

' One Friday, during Holy Communion, He said these words to His unworthy servant, if she is not mistaken : " I promise thee, in the exceeding great (*excessive*) mercy of my Heart, that Its all-powerful love will grant to all those who will receive Holy Communion on nine consecutive first Fridays of the month, the grace of final repentance, not dying in my disfavour and without receiving their sacraments, [my divine Heart] becoming their assured refuge

---

[1] *V.O.*, Letter 86 (II, 395).

at the last moment." '[1]   (*Vie et Œuvres*, 1920, II, 397.)

When setting forth in her writings her revelations, St. Margaret Mary sometimes gives an account of them in a general way with her own thoughts obviously interwoven with them ; at other times she prefaces her statement with some such words as ' He [our Divine Lord] said to me,' and this is what she does in relating the ' Great Promise.'   In such cases the Saint is not giving the exact words of Christ as if they had been dictated to her, for divine communications are not ordinarily made in human speech to their recipient. (Christ did not speak to St. Margaret Mary in a French dialect), they are made either in visions or by supernatural speech,[2] but she is setting forth in human language (and, therefore, with the defects that are inherent in the use of a human instrument to carry out a divine work, e.g. deficiency in literary style, and with the defects that are proper to all human speech) *as directly as possible*, without conscious change, addition, explanation or comment, the divine thought as it had been previously communicated to her in a supernatural way.   Therefore, in the words of the ' Great Promise,' as she wrote them in her letter to Mother de Saumaise, St. Margaret Mary tells us as directly and as correctly as she possibly can—seeing that she must clothe divine thought in human speech—what our Lord conveyed to her ' one Friday during Holy Communion.'

The Saint introduces the words of the Promise by telling us that they were spoken on a Friday ' during

[1] For other versions of the ' Great Promise ' see p. 36.   The words in square brackets do not occur in the original MS. versions of the letter (quite in keeping with the style of St. Margaret Mary), but Gauthey (II, 398) gives them in his text and they are found in the Italian translation (cf. p. 36) and in the version of the Bull of canonization.

[2] See p. 51.

Holy Communion.' It was in such circumstances that Christ was wont to confer His greatest favours on the beloved disciple of His Sacred Heart. He frequently chose a Friday—often a first Friday—when she had received Holy Communion or was praying before the Blessed Sacrament to appear to her and make her a sharer in His divine secrets and confer on her extraordinary favours from the love and mercy of His Heart.

She adds, ' if she is not mistaken.'[1] These words do not imply (as all authorities on the writings of the Saint admit) that she had any real doubt in her mind that Christ had spoken or about what He said. In relating the special favours that Christ conferred on her and His revelations and promises, the Saint frequently uses these words or similar expressions.[2] Her profound humility lead her to speak in a very diffident tone and with great circumspection about such matters. Besides, she was but obeying the orders of her superior and the counsel of her spiritual director. In a *Mémoire* of the Saint which Mother Greyfié—the superior of Paray from 1678 to 1684—wrote in the autumn of 1690, just after Margaret Mary's death, having spoken of the Saint's faithful practice of virtue and exact observance of her duties, she says, ' I told her, however, not to speak of the extraordinary graces which she was receiving except in doubtful terms like " it seems to me," or " if I am not mistaken," and not to rely on herself so firmly that she would not be ready to give way to the judgement of those who were her superiors, or had a right to examine into them [her graces]. She seemed to

---

[1] ' Si elle ne se trompe ' (Letter 86, where she speaks in the third person) ; ' il me semble qu'il me fut dit ' (the version of the *Contemporaines, V.O.*, I, 261).

[2] In letter 86 alone, apart from the words of the Promise, the phrase ' si je ne me trompe ' occurs once, and the expression ' il me semble ' occurs four times.

me always very faithful to this direction.'[1]   In a
letter[2] written to the Saint on September 18, 1686,
by Fr. Rolin, S.J., then her spiritual director, he
lays down certain rules for her guidance.   One of
these (number 9) is ' when you say anything, say
simply, " that is my thought, perhaps I am mistaken " ' ; and in direction 15 he advises her in her
letters to observe the advice that he had given her in
rule 9.   The Saint's humility and obedience in qualifying the accounts of her revelations—not attenuating
them, as a person of timidity or one who was really in
doubt would do—is a confirmation of their genuine
character, and the phrase ' if she is not mistaken '
(which she uses so often in her writings) in no way
weakens the text of the Promise.   ' If the servant of
God,' writes Archbishop Gauthey,[3] ' sometimes uses
phrases expressing doubt or hesitation, it is not
because of uncertainty of mind,[4] but because she was
obeying the advice of her director and of Mother
Greyfié, who had counselled her to use this humble
and modest way of speaking.'

' I promise thee '—the words are perfectly clear
and direct throughout the entire Promise.   The
opening words are unqualified and express a real
promise, for not only do they say so, but they are
followed by the grounds of the promise (' exceeding
great mercy,' and ' all powerful love ') and by its
conditions, Christ promises a favour on condition
that a certain act of devotion is carried out as He
wishes.   There is nothing to prevent our Lord

---

[1] *Mémoire* of Mère Greyfié (*V.O.*, I, 361).
[2] *V.O.*, I, 233, 234.   [3] *V.O.*, II, 18.
[4] This is confirmed by the fact that sometimes what she expresses
in one letter with the phrase ' si je ne me trompe,' she expresses
without qualification in another (e.g. the promise of Christ to bless
the house in which the image of His Heart would be exposed for
veneration ; certain directions given to Fr. Croiset, e.g. in Letters
I and II to him—*V.O.*, II, 517 *sqq.*).

binding Himself *in fidelity* to do something for His creatures. Furthermore, St. Margaret Mary, in her accounts of the various promises that Christ made in connection with devotion to His Sacred Heart (and divine promises are an important feature of that devotion)[1] always assumes that they *are* real promises in the ordinary sense of the word. Had not Christ told her ' I am the Eternal Truth who cannot lie, I am faithful to my promises,'[2] and has she not frequently asserted in her writings this fidelity, for example, in a letter to Fr. Croiset (1689), ' . . . God being faithful to His promises will accomplish the thing Himself rather than leave His work incomplete. For He has always promised to His unworthy servant that He would take care to provide her with all the means necessary to His designs, and that He would not let her want for anything ; and this He has done even beyond His promises.'[3]

' *In the exceeding great mercy of my Heart, Its all-powerful love* '—these words are of the greatest importance in understanding the ' Great Promise.' Such words are not used by Christ as an introduction to any of the other promises that He made to St. Margaret Mary. They clearly indicate that some favour quite outside the accustomed limits of Divine Providence is in question, a favour so great, so unusual, so marvellous—even amid the many ordinary and extraordinary favours that the mercy and love of God are constantly bestowing on men, especially through the devotion to the Sacred Heart—that it springs from a mercy that Christ Himself terms ' excessive ' and brings into play the strongest factor that God can use in His dealings with men, i.e. an ' all-powerful love,' a love that can overcome every difficulty and break down every barrier, and what

---

[1] Cf. pp. 22 *sqq.*   [2] Autobiography (*V.O.*, II, 36).
[3] Letter CXXXI (*V.O.*, II, 537).

greater difficulty or barrier is there for God in relation to men than that which is in question in the
' Great Promise,' the possible resistance of the sinner
to divine grace ? In teaching St. Margaret Mary the
devotion to His Sacred Heart, our Lord repeated over
and over again His desire by means of this devotion
to show mercy *in the greatest abundance* to sinners,
and to *go to extremes* in His desire to try to secure their
love, but in none of His revelations did He speak more
forcibly about, or with greater emphasis on, the
greatness of His mercy and love—what terms could
possibly be stronger ?—than He did in the ' Great
Promise.' If these words by which Christ introduces
the Promise do not mean that He is promising some
grace which is entirely singular, some favour unique
in its greatness, then they mean nothing at all.

' *Will grant to all those who will receive Holy
Communion* ' :

Christ does not limit the Promise, He says ' to all.'
Obviously there is question of only worthy Holy
Communions. The Promise concerns a reward that
is given for a practice that is pleasing to the Sacred
Heart, for Communions of reparation, and so the
condition is a worthy reception of the Blessed Eucharist. Furthermore, the reward is promised for *formal*
compliance with a desire of Christ and so it would
seem essential[1] that the nine Holy Communions

---

[1] This is the view of Fr. Vermeersch (II, 147), of Fr. Estébanez
(p. 31), of Fr. Bainvel (p. 56) and others. Hence it would not suffice
if a person without any thought of the Nine Fridays were in fact to
receive Holy Communion on nine consecutive first Fridays. He
must intend ' to make the Fridays.' It suffices, of course, to *begin*
the Nine Fridays with this intention. The intention will then (if
not retracted) continue virtually until the devotion has been completed. In practice nearly everyone has the express intention of
' making the Fridays ' on each first Friday that he receives Holy
Communion. It is interesting to note that Bishop Languet's account
of the Promise (see p. 38), speaks about the intention (to receive
the grace of final repentance and to honour the Sacred Heart).

should be explicitly offered up to comply with the conditions laid down by our Lord and to fulfil the object of this act of the devotion to the Sacred Heart —which is the same as the object of the entire devotion—i.e. to offer to the Sacred Heart a love of reparation (cf. note 1, p. 74).

' On Nine Consecutive First Fridays of the Month ' :

It is necessary to distinguish clearly between the devotion of the First Friday of the month and the devotion of the Nine First Fridays ; both devotions were taught to St. Margaret Mary by our Lord, but it is the second one that is embodied in the ' Great Promise.' It was in one of the ' great ' apparitions —the one known as the ' third great apparition,' which took place when the Blessed Sacrament was exposed, probably on a First Friday and probably within the octave of Corpus Christi in 1674—that our Lord commanded the Saint to receive Holy Communion on the First Friday of each month in reparation,[1] as one of the great acts of devotion to the Sacred Heart, and she taught this devotion to others and wrote about it many times. That is the devotion of the First Friday—to receive Holy Communion in reparation to the Sacred Heart on any one or more First Fridays.

The devotion of the Nine Fridays consists in an unbroken novena of such Communions and it is to this *novena* that the Promise is attached. Hence the Communions must be made on a first Friday, no other day will do, and for nine first Fridays without a break. What if a person, *through no fault of his own*, is prevented (e.g. by illness, distance from the church, or because the first Friday falls on Good Friday and,

---

[1] Cf. Autobiography (*V.O.*, II, 73) and Letter CXXXIII (*V.O.*, II, 580). See note 1, p. 74 *infra*. The first Friday of the month was chosen by our Lord for a Communion of reparation and for other acts of piety also. (Cf. *V.O.*, II, 282, 330, 383, 398 *note*, 452, 492, 540, and III, 43 *note*, 215.)

therefore, he cannot communicate) from going to
Holy Communion on one of the nine Fridays? As
there is question of a privilege—not of an obligation,
when inability excuses from fulfilment—it would
seem (certainly, if one wants to be on the safe side in
such an important matter) that the conditions must
be fulfilled *to the letter*, and so if the Fridays are
interrupted, even through no fault of the person
concerned, the novena must be begun all over again
and carried through without a break. In practice
this is not a great hardship as most people have the
opportunity of making the Nine Fridays many times
over. Indeed, one of the great fruits of the devotion
is that those who ' make the Fridays ' once, continue
to do so, often for the rest of their life.

Why is Holy Communion to be received for *nine*
Fridays? Why on a Friday? Why on a first Friday
of the month? The answer to these queries is
Christ's secret.[1]   This is what He commanded and

---

[1] It was in the great apparition of 1674 (as St. Margaret Mary
relates in her autobiography—*V.O.*, II, 73—and the *Contemporaines*
repeat the account, *V.O.*, I, 126), that our Lord appointed the first
Friday of the month as a day of special reparation to His Heart and
also taught the Saint the devotion of the Holy Hour. ' You will
receive me,' He said, ' in the Holy Sacrament as often as obedience
will permit you. . . . You will in addition receive Holy Communion
on every first Friday of the month.'   This command is referred to
also (*a*) in the *Mémoire* of the Saint's life that was presented at the
diocesan process for her beatification in 1715 (*V.O.*, I, 461) ; (*b*) by
Sr. Françoise-Rosalie Verchère in her evidence at that process
(*V.O.*, I, 506) ; (*c*) in the *Circulaire* that was sent out from Paray to
the other houses of the Visitation Order, in 1691, after the death of
the Saint, giving an account of her life (*V.O.*, I, 578). Furthermore,
the *Contemporaines* (*V.O.*, I, 245, 246) refer to St. Margaret Mary's
practice of the first Friday Communion when they relate the incident
of our Lord being angry with the Saint's superior for forbidding on
one occasion this Communion to her : and there is reference to
the first Friday Communion in a MS. account (MS. 2) in the Paray
archives of the first practices of the devotion to the Sacred Heart
which were in use in the monastery (*V.O.*, I, 319).

In the long letter (Letter CXXXIII, *V.O.*, II, p. 580), which St.
Margaret Mary wrote in November 1689, to Fr. Croiset, giving an
account of her revelations, she tells of Christ's command and adds

why He did so we do not know ; but we can reverently speculate about some reasons for His choice. The number nine has been associated with religious celebrations from the earliest days of Christianity in connection with memorial services after death (e.g. Mass was offered each day for nine days after the death of a person of high rank). In the earlier part of the Middle Ages the practice arose in certain countries (e.g. France, Spain) of a novena, or special prayers on nine days in preparation for a great festival—at first only for the feast of the Nativity, but later in preparation for other feasts. The prototype of such a novena was none other than that made by our Blessed Lady, the Apostles and the Disciples in preparation for the coming of the Holy Ghost ' when the days of pentecost were accomplished ' (Acts i, 14 ; ii, 1). In the Middle Ages, too, arose another form of novena—the form that concerns us in connection with the ' Great Promise '—the novena of petition, which began by nine days of prayer to certain saints for

the purpose of the first Friday Communion. She was to make this Communion to obtain the grace to bear her heavy sufferings and for other intentions, ' or rather to repair, as far as this is possible for me, the outrages that He has received during the month in the most holy Sacrament.' From the *Contemporaines* (*V.O.*, I, 246) also we learn that the first Friday Communion was to be in reparation for faults against charity, and the MS. account of the first practices of the devotion to the Sacred Heart at Paray gives as the intention for this Communion reparation for sin (*V.O.*, I, 319).

In a letter to Mother de Soudeilles to Moulins, written in 1686 (Letter LII, *V.O.*, II, 330), St. Margaret relates how in the Visitation Convent at Semur (where Mother Greyfié, her former superior at Paray, was now the head), they honour the Sacred Heart by some special act of devotion on all first Fridays ; while in a letter to Mother Dubuysson, written to Moulins in 1689 (Letter CIX, *V.O.*, II, 471), the Saint speaks of an incredible number of people going to Holy Communion in Marseilles every first Friday and mentions that she has heard that in all the Jesuit houses the practice is to be established that the young priests who do not say Mass will go to Holy Communion on every first Friday. The Church has officially recognized the devotion of the First Friday by the singular privilege of permitting the Mass of the Sacred Heart to be celebrated as a *solemn* votive Mass and by the grant of a plenary indulgence.

the recovery of health, and afterwards became a way of urgently seeking for any great favour. In the days of St. Margaret Mary this novena of petition was a widespread popular devotion and this fact may have had something to do with our Lord's choice of a novena of Holy Communions to be made in order to gain a certain signal grace.

That Friday should be a day on which the Sacred Heart desires to be especially honoured naturally follows from the connection of that day with His Sacred Passion. It was on a Friday that Christ conferred most of His favours on St. Margaret Mary; it was Friday—that following the octave of Corpus Christi—that He appointed for the celebration of a feast in honour of His Divine Heart (on the occasion of the ' Great apparition,' within the octave of Corpus Christi, 1675); it was the first Friday of the month that He chose on which He desired that acts of special reparation to His Heart should be made. Was our Lord's choice of the first Friday motived by the fact that *it was on a first Friday*, that of the month of April, *that He was crucified*,[1] and that His Sacred Side was opened by the spear of the soldier and His Heart of flesh was for the first time revealed to human eyes ?

That Holy Communion be received on the first Friday for nine months without a break involves firm faith, an unwavering confidence in God, steadfastness and perseverance (and these—with the state of grace and a proper object sought—are the very conditions of *infallibly efficacious* prayer) and engenders the habit of the regular and frequent reception of the Sacraments of Penance and the Blessed Eucharist, which is such an important factor in obtaining final perseverance.

[1] According to the best authorities, Christ was crucified either in the year 30 or 33. In those years the fourteenth Nisan occurred on a Friday—on a first Friday—on April 7 in 30, on April 3 in 33.

' The Grace of Final Repentance ' :

What our Lord promised in return for the nine Communions of reparation is really *one single favour*, i.e., to die in the state of grace—not to die in the state of mortal sin (' not dying in my disfavour '). The reception of ' their sacraments ' is promised only in this connection and therefore *conditionally*, i.e. in so far as this reception is essential to dying in the state of grace[1] (the actual reception of a sacrament is the ordinary, but not the sole means of obtaining the remission of grave sin). Having His Divine Heart as ' their assured refuge at the last moment,' is simply the cause or the effect—according to the point of view—of dying in the state of grace.

Two classes of people secure the grace of final perseverance—of dying in the state of grace—i.e. the good, those who habitually live in the state of grace, and some sinners, those who though they do not live habitually in God's friendship and may be found in mortal sin at the approach of death, are given the grace of repentance before death finishes the journey of life. Final perseverance in reference to such sinners is called ' final repentance.' It involves two special graces—(*a*) the grace to repent, i.e. to be sorry for sin with a sorrow which is sincere, supernatural, universal, and sovereign, and to take the steps requisite for its remission—and (*b*) the coming of death when the guilt of grave sin has been forgiven and while the soul remains in the state of grace. Only such repentance would be ' final.' That the ' Great Promise' not only includes sinners but is

[1] This interpretation of the words ' not dying . . . without receiving their sacraments,' is a reasonable one and is adopted by Frs. Boubée, Coubé, Estébanez, Galeazzi, Guillaume, Le Bachelet, Lejeune, McDonnell, Ramière, Redon, Smit, Suau, Terrien and Vermeersch (Cf. Estébanez, p. 39). Even the grammatical construction of the wording of the ' Promise ' with its dependent clauses, ' *ne mourant*,' etc., (cf. p. 36), suggests this interpretation (cf. Galeazzi, p. 52).

G

made entirely in their favour is shown by the phrases in which the promised grace is described : ' final repentance,' ' not dying in my disfavour,' ' without receiving their sacraments.' The habitually good do not need the grace of ' final *repentance*,' for they are in the state of grace (they do, of course, need the grace of final perseverance—which even they cannot merit in the strict and proper sense of the term ' merit,' but which they can *infallibly* obtain by prayer and good works), nor are they in proximate danger of dying in God's disfavour, nor do they need ' their sacraments ' for salvation. Besides, in the case of the habitually good, death in the friendship of God would not be that very special grace flowing from the ' exceeding great mercy,' and effected by ' the all-powerful love ' of the Sacred Heart that the ' Great Promise ' envisages. Indeed, a very special care for sinners is a leading feature of the entire devotion of the Sacred Heart, which our Lord described as a ' last effort ' of His love on behalf of sinners.

' *And without receiving their Sacraments.*'—A superficial reading of the ' Great Promise ' suggests that by this phrase our Lord promises to all who make the ' Nine Fridays ' (*a*) an additional favour distinct from the grace of final repentance, (*b*) the reception of what are called ' the last sacraments '— the sacraments which are administered in preparation for death, i.e. ordinarily, Penance, Holy Viaticum and Extreme Unction, (*c*) in every hypothesis. Such an interpretation is not borne out by a careful study of the words. In all the extant versions of the Promise the same phrase is given *recevoir leurs sacrements*. Some writers think that the key to the meaning lies in the word *leurs*, and that ' their ' sacraments means those sacraments which in any particular case may be needed to secure the grace of a happy death. This interpretation cannot be deduced from the word *leurs*, for *leurs sacrements* in the days of St. Margaret Mary was a popular phrase meaning simply, the 'last Sacraments,' and there is no special meaning in the word *leurs*. Thus the Saint herself in her autobiography,[1] relates that through her intercession with our Lord one of the sisters of the community of Paray, who was dying and in a lethargy, was enabled to receive 'her sacraments' (*ses sacrements*), and the same expression is used by Mother Greyfié[2] in her account of this incident. The term 'ses sacrements' is used more than once, too, in the accounts of the Saint's own death.[3] The authentic Italian translation of the Promise gives simply *i sagramenti* ('the sacraments') and the account of the Promise in the bull of canonization of St. Margaret Mary (1920) has *sanctis non receptis sacramentis*[4] ('without receiving the holy sacraments').

To understand the meaning of 'their sacraments' it is necessary *to study the context* in which the phrase occurs. It is quite evident that the favour which our Lord promises in return for the making of the Fridays—the great favour springing from 'the exceeding great mercy' and 'all-powerful love' of His Sacred Heart—is the grace of death in the friendship of God. This is the clear meaning of three out of the four phrases that make up the actual promise : 'the grace of final repentance,' 'not dying in my disfavour,' my Heart 'becoming their assured refuge at the last moment'—all these mean the very same thing, *one* grace (the grace of a happy death), and the Saint repeats what the grace is in different forms so that there can be no mistake about what is meant. Now it is not in isolation that the phrase ' and without

---

[1] *V.O.*, II, 110.
[2] *V.O.*, I, 384.
[3] e.g. *V.O.*, I, 312, 490.
[4] Cf. p. 36.

receiving their sacraments' occurs, but embedded in the three phrases that all go to express the same thing, i.e. to die in the state of grace. And so the most reasonable interpretation of the phrase is not that it expresses an *additional* favour (the reception of the sacraments), but that it is all part of the one grace, the grace of a happy death, and therefore means that those who ' make the Fridays ' will receive *such sacraments as may be necessary in any particular case to secure for them the favour of dying in the friendship of God*. The sacraments are but a means to an end, the end being grace ; and the actual reception of them is not even an indispensable means to this end. The reception of Penance by desire—when the actual reception is not possible—can secure the state of grace. Accordingly, it does not follow from the words of the Promise that the ' last sacraments ' will be received by every single person who has ' made the Fridays.' What does follow is that a person who has duly ' made the Fridays ' will receive such sacraments (and they may be none at all) as may be necessary in his particular case to secure that he dies in the state of grace.

It is sometimes urged against the authenticity of the ' Great Promise ' or against interpreting it literally that persons who have ' made the Fridays ' have died suddenly and without the last sacraments. Granted the truth of this it is not a valid objection against the Promise for—(*a*) the sacraments may not have been necessary to secure for such persons death in the state of grace, (*b*) the Promise does not say that the sacraments will be received *immediately* before death. Even if the Promise guaranteed the reception of ' their sacraments ' in every case (which it does not), it would be perfectly fulfilled by the reception of the sacraments—by persons who die suddenly—*quite a long time before their death*. Perhaps months before the unexpected call came they had received the sacraments and their effect, sanctifying grace, had remained in the soul to the moment of death. (c) In any particular case how do we know that the person who died suddenly had *duly* fulfilled the conditions of the Promise, i.e. the *worthy* reception of Holy Communion on nine consecutive first Fridays? Hence, the sudden death of a person who had ' made the Nine Fridays ' without receiving the last sacraments shortly before, is not a valid objection to the ' Great Promise.'

In any event, whatever difficulty may arise about the meaning of the words ' and without receiving their sacraments '—were they part of the original Promise or not[1]—the Promise itself and the main revelation which it embodies, remains untouched. Its authenticity has been proved by satisfactory and (we claim) convincing evidence and its literal interpretation[2] is not rendered impossible, or even improbable, because a fully satisfactory explanation of one subsidiary clause in the Promise may yet be wanting.

[1] See the appendix which follows immediately.
[2] See chapter VIII, *infra*.

APPENDIX

PÈRE A. HAMON, S.J., has another explanation[1] of the difficult words of the 'Great Promise' *and without receiving their sacraments*. He thinks that these words (which certainly do not seem to fit too well into the sentence which relates the Promise) are a gloss which was added, quite in good faith, by St. Margaret Mary. When she wrote her account of the Promise—which she had received either in vision or by supernatural speech[2]— she had a perfectly clear idea of what Christ had communicated to her, she understood clearly that He had promised the grace of final repentance in return for a novena of communions made on consecutive first Fridays. Now her notion of the grace of final repentance (she was no theologian) was the grace of receiving the last sacraments, ' their sacraments,' at the approach of death—this is the idea of most Catholics who often do not understand that the sacraments are but a means to an end—or, at least, the idea of the reception of the sacraments was in her mind inseparably, indeed almost necessarily, connected with the idea of a happy death, and so when she came to express in human language the divine idea (the Promise), and was no longer directly under the divine influence in the way that she was at the time that she received the revelation, she added—not intending to modify in any way the divine message—the words ' and without receiving their sacraments.'

Père Hamon is fully satisfied about the historical

[1] Père Hamon outlined his view in recent private letters to the present writer (April 1934), and has graciously given permission of the publication of his theory. It has been set forth at some length for the benefit of readers of this book and Père Hamon has approved of the outline which is given above.

[2] See pp. 51 *sqq.*

authenticity of the ' Great Promise ' (see p. 47) ; he is satisfied, too, with its theological soundness and he believes that it should be accepted literally (see p. 93), but understanding that all private revelations need critical examination to reach exactly the divine thought when it has been clothed in human language,[1] he considers that such an examination of the words of the ' Great Promise ' at least *strongly suggests* that our Lord in His communication to the Saint did not speak about the reception of the last sacraments. This was added, in perfect good faith, by St. Margaret Mary in her endeavour to express in ordinary human speech the divine thought.

Père Hamon concludes the exposition of his theory with these striking words[2]—' Mon interprétation a ses avantages et ses inconvénients. Cela est certain, et on peut ne pas l'admettre, la grande promesse reste avec toute la certitude morale que l'on peut donner aux révélations de Paray-le-Monial. J'y crois de tout mon cœur et de tout mon esprit.'

---

[1] Cf. pp. 53, 62, 68.   [2] Letter of May 16, 1934.

CHAPTER VIII

THE MEANING OF THE 'GREAT PROMISE'

(A) *Some Interpretations That Are Not Acceptable.*

AT the present day few—if any—authorities seriously question the authenticity, either historical or theological, of the 'Great Promise.' There is not quite the same unanimity about the *meaning* of the Promise, which is an entirely different question.[1]

That the Promise is susceptible of *an* orthodox interpretation is evident from the ·fact that the Church found nothing in the writings of St. Margaret Mary—which included the letter in which the Promise is given—'worthy of theological censure,'[2] that the Promise is embodied in the Bull of Canonization of the Saint,[3] and the practice of the 'Nine Fridays' is widespread throughout the Church.

Some writers explain the 'Great Promise' by saying that a practice which is so salutary, a devotion which is so solid as the 'making of the Nine Fridays,' involving as it does the persevering reception of the sacraments, the making of many sacrifices to carry out the condition of a worthy Holy Communion made on nine successive first Fridays, the break with sin and habits of sin that it requires in the case of sinners (and the Promise is primarily concerned with

---

[1] Some 'popular' writers mix up in a very confusing way the two entirely distinct questions of the *authenticity* and the *interpretation* of the 'Great Promise.'

[2] S.R.C. September 26, 1827.   [3] *A.A.S.*, 1920, p. 503.

them) and all the rest results in a virtuous life and continuance in good, by God's grace, and therefore—in the end—the grace of final perseverance.[1] This explanation is not tenable. It eviscerates the Promise and really makes it mean nothing. According to this view it is to the reception of the sacraments nine times at regular intervals that the good result—death in the state of grace—is really due. If this be so why should not the same effect be expected from such devotions as the eight first Saturdays in honour of our Lady (a devotion which has been indulgenced by the Church and which involves the reception of Penance and Holy Communion for eight months consecutively) or similar approved practices? If the good effect—death in the friendship of God—is due to the *intrinsic* virtue of the devotion of the Nine Fridays, where is the peculiar grace that ' the exceeding great mercy ' and ' all-powerful love ' of Christ is giving in return for this special act of honour, love and reparation to His Sacred Heart? Such an interpretation of the Promise is quite inadequate.

Others, fearing to accept the words of the ' Great Promise ' literally, as they stand, because they think that there are theological reasons[2] why this may not be done or because they fear the consequences in practice of the literal interpretation of such an immense favour, attenuate the meaning of the Promise. They hold that in addition to the conditions which were laid down by our Lord, other conditions, either general[3] (i.e. the ordinary economy of

---

[1] While Fr. H. Thurston (in *The Month*, 1903) gives little space to the question of the *meaning* of the ' Great Promise ' and does not commit himself definitely to any view on it, he *seems* (p. 648) to incline to such an opinion as the above. So also, apparently, Fr. Nix (p. 175, note 2).

[2] These reasons are dealt with on pp. 98 *sqq*.

[3] So, e.g. Père A. Michel in *Dictionnaire de Théologie* (1933), CV, col. 1302.

salvation—the observance of the commandments, the practice of virtue and so forth) or particular, must be understood. If the ' Great Promise ' simply means that, in some vague general way, special grace leading to a happy death will be given to those who make the Nine Fridays *provided that* they observe the general conditions for salvation which are appointed for all men, then it means really nothing. To any practice of piety, however trivial, one might—even infallibly—attach the grace of final perseverance, *if* this practice involves as one of its understood conditions the fulfilment of all that is laid down by the law of God for the attainment of salvation.

Those who think that some special condition must be understood—added to what the Promise states—do not agree as to what this condition is. Thus Fr. Smit, S.J., in the Dutch *Messenger of the Sacred Heart*, requires that a certain degree of fervour (what degree cannot be ascertained !) in making the Fridays should be attained ;[1] Fr. le Bachelet[2]—with whom Canon Truptin seems to agree[3]—requires that the person who makes the Nine Fridays must not subsequently sin gravely out of presumption,[4] relying on the Promise. The objection to such views is that they add gratuitously, without cogent reason, to the conditions laid down by Christ and thus change and attentuate His promise. Our Lord said nothing about *fervent* Holy Communions. Besides, His promise was made primarily in favour of *sinners*, not for the benefit of the fervent ; it was made for the many (' all those who . . .'), not for a few elect souls.

[1] *Maandrozen* (Dec. 1904, Jan. 1905, Feb. 1906).

[2] p. 389. Subsequently Le Bachelet seems to have changed his opinion and to have adopted the literal interpretation of the Promise in reviewing Galeazzi's book (see p. xvi) in *Études*, 1911, pp. 108 *sqq.* (cf. *infra*, p. 92, note 1).

[3] p. 302.

[4] The question of presumption is dealt with on pp. 104 *sqq.*

Nor did Christ declare or suggest that subsequent sin,[1] even from presumption, would annul the Promise—if it did the Promise would be of little or no value. To add to the conditions which were laid down by our Lord is quite unnecessary,[2] and to do so is not only gratuitous, but eviscerates or seriously attenuates the Promise. It ceases to be a singular favour springing from the 'exceeding great mercy' and 'all-powerful love' of the Sacred Heart of Jesus.

Some writers while they do not add fresh conditions for the attainment of the favour of a happy death to those which are embodied in the 'Great Promise,' fearing to accept the Promise as it stands, see in it but the promise of an extra grace at the end of life. They will not admit that this grace will be an 'efficacious' grace[3] or, if they are forced to admit that it will be (for Christ says quite simply and clearly that He will grant the grace of final repentance, repeats the promise by the words 'not dying in my disfavour,' and confirms it with the words 'becoming their secure refuge at the last moment '), they maintain that the giving of this grace is only *probable*—more or less probable according to the particular view of each author. Thus, Bishop Languet in his *Life of Saint Margaret Mary* (1729), speaking of the devotion says, 'leading her (St. Margaret Mary) to hope for the grace of final repentance,' etc.; Petrovits, 'the reception of the promised graces *may be humbly expected*' (p. 263); Truptin, 'this promise contains a very great probability of salvation' (p. 293). Such an interpretation of the 'Great Promise' is not acceptable. It deprives it of its full

---

[1] That subsequent sin does not render useless the making of the Nine Fridays is apparent from the very words of the Promise which speaks of final *repentance* and repentance supposes sin.

[2] See the defence of the literal interpretation of the Promise which follows (pp. 89 *sqq.*).

[3] See p. 89.

and proper meaning. Christ did not say that to all those who will receive Holy Communion on nine consecutive first Fridays of the month, He ' may ' give, or ' probably ' or ' most probably,' would give the grace of final repentance. He said : ' I *promise* thee, in the exceeding great mercy of my Heart, Its all-powerful love, *will* grant . . . the grace of final repentance,' and what He promises He can and does accomplish.

Another interpretation that has been given to the ' Great Promise '[1] is this—our Lord promises the grace of final repentance, He lays down as a condition the making of nine worthy Holy Communions on consecutive first Fridays, a practice which of its nature will help much towards the attainment of final perseverance, He attaches to the practice a very special blessing which will facilitate perseverance, but it is for us *to co-operate* with this grace, and if we fail to do so (particularly if we are guilty of sin or tepidity after having ' made the Fridays ') final repentance will not result. In other words the Promise offers a great grace, but, only a ' sufficient ' grace[2]—one that will (or rather may) fail in its effect owing to want of co-operation on our part. Such an interpretation eviscerates the ' Great Promise ' and is not acceptable, nor is it forced upon us (as its advocates seem to think) by theological difficulties against the more generous, the literal, interpretation of the Promise.[3] Unless the grace which the Promise guarantees is an ' efficacious ' grace—a grace, co-operation with which is infallibly, though freely, secured—it could not be described as a grace flowing from ' the exceeding great mercy ' and ' all-powerful love ' of the Sacred Heart.

[1] By, e.g. Père A. Guillaume, S.J., in *Les Promesses du Sacré-Cœur* (1899), pp. 138 *sqq.*
[2] See pp. 89 *sqq.*   [3] *Ibid.*

(B) *The True Interpretation of the 'Great Promise.'*

The primary and fundamental rule of all interpretation of the words of another is that they are to be accepted in their *ordinary, natural, obvious* meaning unless good reason can be given for not so accepting them. The words of the 'Great Promise' are the words of St. Margaret Mary setting forth the divine promise. They are quite simple and clear, there is nothing mysterious or obscure about them. The thought which these words express is perfectly clear, too. When our Lord makes a revelation to a human agent He neither exaggerates nor minimises, but—when He does not wish to 'speak in parables' —plainly expresses His thought in language that He knows will be understood by those to whom He gives His message and secures that they will set it forth in a way comprehensible to those for whom His message is intended (cf. p. 52). He said : ' I promise thee, in the exceeding great mercy of my Heart, that Its all-powerful love will grant to all those who will receive Holy Communion on nine consecutive first Fridays of the month, the grace of final repentance. . . .' Unless good and sufficient reasons are forthcoming against attaching to these words their obvious, natural meaning, they should be interpreted literally—understood as they stand. When they are so accepted the meaning of the 'Great Promise' is that to those who comply with the conditions which He has laid down Christ will give an ' *efficacious* ' (actual) grace which will secure for them the state of (sanctifying) grace—repentance, if need be—at the hour of death.[1] To everyone God gives ' *sufficient* '

[1] In a letter to her brother (1689), St. Margaret Mary speaks of the devotion to the Sacred Heart as ' a last effort of the love of the Lord towards sinners to draw them to repentance and to give them in abundance His efficacious and sanctifying graces to procure their salvation, many of whom will be held back from the abyss of perdition by this means ' (*V.O.*, II, 445).

grace for salvation, i.e. actual grace which is truly sufficient to secure justification and, therefore, salvation, provided that the recipient co-operates with it.   To everyone God does *not* give the 'efficacious' grace of salvation, i.e. such actual grace as is not only truly sufficient to secure salvation, but with which, in point of fact (and God knows this beforehand), the recipient will co-operate, and thus the grace *infallibly* secures its end or purpose (in this case final perseverance, salvation).   To *all* sinners God gives 'sufficient' grace to repent; to *some* sinners He gives 'efficacious' grace to repent, i.e. grace which secures the co-operation of the sinner and will *certainly* obtain its effect.   God can so overcome the resistance of the will to grace—can so deal with the hardness and obstinacy of the sinner—that the sinner *will* accept the grace, accept it freely, yet certainly. To some sinners God gives such an 'efficacious' grace ; to some He gives it at the close of their life and accompanies it with the favour of dying after justification and before the commission of further grave sin, this is the great grace of 'final repentance.' God is quite free to grant or withhold such an 'efficacious' grace—God is the master of His graces, 'He hath mercy on whom He will, and whom He will He hardeneth.'[1]   He may if He chooses attach the granting of such a grace to compliance with certain conditions ; He may declare these conditions and promise the grace beforehand to those who fulfil them.   This is precisely what He has done in the case of the 'Great Promise.'   To those who receive Holy Communion for nine consecutive first Fridays to honour His Sacred Heart, He has promised the grace of final repentance, an 'efficacious' grace— one that will *certainly*, though quite freely, secure the co-operation of the sinner and will *infallibly* result

[1] Romans ix, 18.

in justification and salvation. To repeat—God can so overwhelm, if it be necessary, the will of any sinner with His grace as to secure that he will quite freely, yet with absolute certainty, co-operate with the grace and secure its effect, in this case final repentance. This He has promised to do, if it be necessary, for those who have ' made the Nine Fridays.'[1]

The literal meaning of the ' Great Promise,' then, is this—in the words of Fr. Vermeersch, S.J., the eminent theologian—' Those who will communicate on nine consecutive first Fridays with the required dispositions will have, all of them, the grace of final perseverance. And, accordingly, the faithful who, with a good will, do their best to fulfil this condition are morally certain of their salvation ' (II, 144).

So explained, the ' Great Promise ' is indeed great. It is one of many promises—the most precise and definite of them all—made in connection with the devotion to the Sacred Heart, the leading characteristic of which, in reference to men, is Christ's great love for sinners and His ardent desire to show mercy to them and to draw them to His love by a love and compassion God-like in their munificence. The ' Great Promise,' when accepted literally, is indeed a grace worthy of ' the exceeding great mercy ' and ' all-powerful love ' of the Divine Heart.

Among the leading modern authorities who accept and defend the literal interpretation of the Promise are Frs. Aloisi-Masella, S.J. (pp. 13 sqq.), Bainvel, S.J. (pp. 55–7 and Dictionnaire de Théologie, III, 331), Boubée, Cathrein, Estébanez, S.J. (pp. 90 sqq.),

---

[1] It is important to note that the ' making of the Fridays ' is not the cause (as a sacrament is the cause of sanctifying grace and of a right to actual grace) but the condition of ' the efficacious ' grace of final repentance. The cause is ' the exceeding great mercy ' and the ' all-powerful love ' of the Sacred Heart.

Galeazzi, S.J. (pp. 42 *sqq.*), Hamon, S.J. (I, 434 and III, 329), Hättenschwiller, S.J., Le Bachelet[1] (*Études*, 1911, pp. 108 *sqq.*), McDonnell, S.J. (pp. 146 *sqq.*), O'Loan (*Irish Ecclesiastical Record*, 1895, Vol. XVI, p. 543), Vermeersch, S.J. (II, 137 *sqq.*).   Fr. Estébanez[2] cites Fr. Ramière, S.J., l'abbé Coubé and Canon Lejeune also as defenders of the literal interpretation of the Promise.   Indeed, since the clear and courageous lead which Fr. Vermeersch gave, in 1903, in accepting and cogently defending the literal interpretation we think it is true to say that few writers have adopted any other view.

While certain authors have been, we believe, too timid in their interpretation of the ' Great Promise,' others—writers of the popular type, whose zeal is not always according to knowledge—have read into the Promise meanings which it cannot bear.[3] While the Promise guarantees, we contend, a grace of the greatest value and of the highest importance—the grace of final repentance—it does not promise perseverance in good, preservation from mortal sin, during or after the ' making of the Nine Fridays ' ; nor does it guarantee one against sudden death or ensure the reception of the ' last sacraments ' in any hypothesis or immediately before death.

To the timid, who shrink from the acceptance of

---

[1] Fr. le Bachelet in *Études*, 1901 (pp. 385 *sqq.*), favoured a restricted interpretation of the ' Great Promise.'   Fr. Vermeersch replied to his arguments in *Études*, 1903 (pp. 593 *sqq.*).   That Fr. le Bachelet changed his opinion and later accepted the literal interpretation of the Promise is shown by his remarks on Fr. Galeazzi's book in *Études*, 1911 (pp. 108 *sqq.*   Cf. Bainvel, p. 55 , note 2).

[2] pp. 73 and 90.

[3] Petrovits (pp. 215 *sqq.* and p. 256) quite rightly objects to some of the exaggerated interpretations that have been given to the Promise.   He is not, however, himself always quite accurate in his accusations of unfounded interpretations against other writers (cf., e.g., his version of the statements of *Catéchisme de la Dévotion au Sacré-Cœur*, with the actual French text of the catechism given in a note on the same page, p. 216).

the words of the 'Great Promise' in their natural, obvious, literal sense, we commend these words[1] of Père Hamon, S.J., one of the leading modern authorities on devotion to the Sacred Heart : ' Often the Saint (Margaret Mary) affirms that those who are devoted to the Sacred Heart will not perish. The general statement assumes a concrete form here, it is embodied in a definite practice : final perseverance is assured to those who will have received Holy Communion on nine consecutive first Fridays of the month. This promise is something unique ; there are other promises that are somewhat similar, but they are clearly distinguished from it. If we are surprised, if our soul, in wonder but ever distrustful, fears to rest in such a generous and divine hope, let us read slowly the clear and grave words. It is a God who makes the promise ; there is question of neither merit nor justice ; it is a great wave of love that breaks upon the earth and covers it over, an excess of love, one of those unexpected divine interventions which fill men and angels with awe. "Exceeding great mercy," "all-powerful love" ; such strong words far surpass any ordinary promise and afford a foundation for even the most sanguine hopes. *Misericordias Domine in æternum cantabo.*[2] It is for us to sing for ever the mercies of the Lord ; it is for us to give to the "Great Promise" the widest interpretation that theology allows ; that is its meaning or else it means nothing at all.'

(C) *Objections to the Literal Interpretation of the 'Great Promise.'*

Some have hesitated or even refused to accept the literal and obvious meaning of our Lord's words in the 'Great Promise' either for historical reasons or,

---

[1] *Histoire*, III, 328.
[2] Psalm 88, v. 2 ; a constant prayer of St. Margaret Mary.

H

much more, because they think that the literal interpretation of the Promise is in conflict with the teaching of the Church on certain points or because they fear that, in practice, it would lead to serious abuses. ' Undoubtedly the watering down of the Promise by the timid,' writes Fr. Vermeersch, S.J.,[1] ' is dictated by a laudable intention, but fear of the truth has always seemed to us a sorry defence of good. Such a way of acting sometimes saves laborious research, but it is only an expedient which is always doubtful and often dangerous. Let us rather seek from truth itself weapons of a better temper. Often it will suffice to present the truth clearly. Truth does harm only if it is misunderstood or badly presented.'

Objections have been or may be made to the literal interpretation of the ' Great Promise ' on historical grounds or for theological reasons.

(I) *Objections on Historical Grounds.*

(1) Bishop Languet, one of the earliest biographers of St. Margaret Mary, in his *La Vie de la Vénérable Mère Marguerite-Marie,*[2] which was published in 1729, gives this account of the ' Great Promise ' : ' In another letter she prescribes a practice to honour the Heart of Jesus Christ ; a practice which was familiar to her and which our Lord had suggested to her, making her to hope for the grace of final repentance and that of receiving the sacraments of the Church before dying, for those who observe it. It was to make a novena of Communions for this intention and to honour the Heart of Jesus Christ, making each of these Communions on each first Friday of the month for nine consecutive months.''[3]

---

[1] II, 151.   [2] See above, p. 30.
[3] *La Vie*, Bk. VII, pp. 241-2.

It will be seen from Bishop Languet's words that his interpretation of the Promise was that those 'who make the Fridays' may '*hope for*'—but, apparently, cannot be certain of receiving—the grace of final repentance. Hence, the Promise is not to be interpreted literally.

Reply. (i) In *La Vie* Mgr. Languet does not profess to give the actual words of the Promise, quoting St. Margaret Mary. He merely gives an *account* of the Promise and *his* idea of its interpretation[1] and the arguments which we have given above against any attenuated interpretation of the Promise are valid against this modified interpretation of Languet. (Recall that the Saint did not give an account of the Promise, or suggest any interpretation of it. She set forth in her letter to Mother de Saumaise directly and simply the mind of Christ as it was revealed to her.)

(ii) That Mgr. Languet would tone down somewhat the 'Great Promise' in his account of it is exactly what we should expect. Because of the violent opposition which was offered in his day, not only by Jansenists, Gallicans and free-thinkers, but even by many of the Catholic clergy (including bishops) and faithful, to the new form of devotion to the Sacred Heart, it was with great difficulty that Languet was persuaded by the religious of Paray to publish his *Life of Margaret Mary Alacoque.* She was then an obscure nun, regarded by many as a visionary and laughed at ; he was a very distinguished ecclesiastic (who was, however, somewhat timid in character and had been much calumniated), a member of the French

---

[1] Petrovits (p. 186 and p. 246) while endeavouring to argue against the literal interpretation from the words of Languet has to admit that these words are 'not a quotation of the original promise, but only an interpretation of it given by the author.'

Academy with a great reputation as a savant, and the publication of the Life brought on him scorn, ridicule and even scurrilous attacks. The entire devotion to the Sacred Heart as revealed to St. Margaret Mary, was then in its infancy, it was little understood and often gravely misrepresented, and it was regarded with suspicion by many and violently attacked by some. Hence the first writers about the devotion and about the Saint of Paray wrote not only with great circumspection, but timidly and hesitatingly—with good reason. They had a tendency to change the thought of St. Margaret Mary, not in substance, but by weakening it somewhat.[1] To have set forth the 'Great Promise' exactly in the terms in which it is stated by the Saint would have aroused further bitter opposition and given the enemies of devotion to the Sacred Heart a new weapon of offence.[2] Hence the somewhat attenuated account of the Promise which Mgr. Languet gives is not a cogent argument against its literal interpretation. That, in the circumstances, the Bishop of Soissons should make any mention of the Promise is a clear indication that he was satisfied as to its authenticity (and this in the lifetime of Margaret Mary's contemporaries) and must have been impressed by its importance.

(2) During the Apostolic Process, in 1843–4, preliminary to the Beatification (1864) of St. Margaret Mary, the question of the 'Great Promise'

---

[1] Cf. pp. 40 *sqq.* above. Père Hamon in an article in *Études* (1902, Vol, 91, pp. 724 *sqq.*) examines the early Lives of the Saint and shows how writers like Languet and Croiset had a tendency (owing to the circumstances of the time when they wrote) to water down the thought of Margaret Mary. 'Ils ne se montrent pas suffisamment historiens, ils veulent surtout édifier.'

[2] Even in our own time it is curious to note the intemperate attacks that have been sometimes made on the 'Great Promise' (e.g. some of the letters that were contributed to a controversy on the subject that took place in the pages of *The Tablet* in 1903, 1904 and 1939).

was discussed.[1] As private revelations which contain assurance of salvation are especially open to suspicion (owing to the Catholic teaching about the uncertainty of salvation, the impossibility of meriting *de condigno* final perseverance and other such questions), the *Promotor Fidei* or 'Devil's Advocate' (A. M. Frattini), in his *Animadversiones supra Dubio de Virtutibus* (§ 80), formally took exception to the 'Great Promise.' In his reply to this, Mgr. Arnaldi,[2] the Postulator of the Cause, argued that it is presumed that in all such promises it is implied that God's law is diligently kept, that they amount to no more than an assurance of special graces, that the veneration of the Sacred Heart is but a special form of the love of God and that any practice of this love essentially includes the keeping of the commandments, and so forth. In other words the Postulator met the objection based on the 'Great Promise' by favouring an attenuated interpretation of it.

Reply. (i) Mgr. Arnaldi's attenuated interpretation is his own personal opinion, nothing more, and his view is answered by the arguments which we have adduced against any interpretation that departs from the natural and obvious meaning of the words.

(ii) The question of the 'Great Promise' was but a small detail in the big question of the examination of the virtues of St. Margaret Mary. It was dealt with merely in a passing and very incomplete way. It was not the intention of either the *Promotor Fidei* or the Postulator to discuss the question of the authenticity of the Promise or its meaning as a matter of

[1] The writings of the Saint (including Letter 86, with the words of the Promise underlined—cf. p. 63 above) had been examined previously and pronounced by a decree of the Congregation of S. Rites (September 26, 1827), free of anything that would 'merit theological censure.'

[2] *Responsio ad Animadversiones*, § 353.

importance or of interest in itself.[1] Hence the Promotor contented himself with merely touching on the matter in the course of a long series of objections, great and small, and the Postulator, skilled advocate that he was, took the line of least resistance in his reply, avoided the larger issue of the real meaning of the Promise (which was then unknown except to the few who had studied the writings of St. Margaret Mary, not then published) and contented himself with giving a reply which sufficed to meet the scruples of the Promotor (who, clearly, must not have seen in the Promise any very strong argument against the cause of St. Margaret Mary). Hence, the opinion of Mgr. Arnaldi cannot be regarded as a cogent argument against the literal interpretation of the Promise.

(II) *Objections on Theological Grounds.*

The theological objections which have been or may be made against the literal interpretation of the ' Great Promise ' arise, mainly, from the Catholic teaching about the uncertainty and gratuitous character of final perseverance (final repentance).

(1) If the Promise be literally accepted it means that those who have ' made the Nine Fridays ' are certain of final repentance. But this conclusion is contrary to the doctrine of the Council of Trent which condemns those who hold that, apart from a special revelation, they can be certain of final perseverance.

Reply. What the Council of Trent (Session VI, canon 16) condemned was to hold that anyone could

---

[1] The Postulator classed the ' Great Promise ' with promises made in recommending the Rosary, the brown scapular, etc. This shows that he did not devote to it any very special study. The ' Great Promise ' is quite different from such other promises and is not be classed with them except in a very rough and ready classification.

be certain (apart from special revelation) with ' *an absolute and infallible certainty*,' that he will obtain ' that great gift of final perseverance.' Now the certainty that we have (*a*) that the ' Great Promise ' was made to St. Margaret Mary, has been correctly transmitted to and interpreted by us, or that (*b*) those who have ' made the Nine Fridays ' have duly observed the conditions of the Promise (were, *e.g.* in the state of grace when making each of the nine Communions), is not ' an absolute and infallible ' certainty—the certainty of divine faith—but a *moral* certainty, *i.e.* the certainty that is based on entirely satisfactory, but human evidence—the certainty of historical evidence which is based on excellent grounds, perhaps on unanswerable arguments, for the truth in question and excludes all prudent and reasonable fear of the contrary, but does not exclude absolutely even the *possibility* of error. Hence, even those who have ' made the Nine Fridays ' must still ' with fear and trembling work out their salvation.'[1] The same Council of Trent, while condemning presumption regarding salvation, equally condemned those who hold that we cannot persevere ' with the special help of God ' (canon 22), and taught that we ought to have ' a most firm hope ' in the help of God to persevere (chap. 13); and theologians teach that final perseverance can be *infallibly* obtained by prayer.

(2) If the ' Great Promise ' be interpreted literally it means a divine promise of final repentance attached to the performance of a certain act. Hence, it means that the grace of final repentance can be merited. But this is contrary to Catholic teaching. Hence the ' Great Promise ' may not be accepted literally.

Reply. It is contrary to Catholic teaching to hold that the grace of final repentance can be merited in

[1] Philippians ii, 12.

the strict sense (*de condigno*—in justice)[1]; it is not contrary to Catholic teaching to affirm that final repentance can be merited in a broad sense (*de congruo*—in equity). Furthermore, it is not contrary to Catholic teaching to maintain that the grace of final repentance can be merited *de congruo* and *infallibly*, *if* there is a divine promise attaching this grace to the performance of any good work.[2] It does not necessarily follow from interpreting the 'Great Promise' literally that the grace of final repentance can be merited in the strict sense (*de condigno*), but it does follow that it can be merited in the broad sense (*de congruo*) and *infallibly*, and this is not contrary to Catholic doctrine. Not from the intrinsic value of the good work (nine worthy Holy Communions) and the ordination of God binding Himself to reward it with the grace of final repentance does the certain attainment of this grace follow from the Promise, but from the *divine generosity and mercy* attaching the favour to this particular good work (cf. note, p. 91).

(3) Theologians commonly teach that the grace of final perseverance (or of final repentance) is entirely gratuitous. But the 'Great Promise,' if accepted literally, implies that final perseverance can be merited at least in equity (*de congruo*) and so is to be attributed to the 'making of the Fridays.' Hence, the grace of final repentance is not gratuitous. But this conclusion is inadmissible. Therefore the Promise may not be taken literally.

Reply. (i) To say that the grace of final repen-

---

[1] The question of merit *de condigno* cannot arise in connection with the Promise for such merit requires the state of grace, while the grace of final repentance supposes the presence of grave sin.

[2] As this book is not a theological treatise on grace and merit, the proofs of these statements are not given. They may be found in any standard work on grace and in connection with the 'Great Promise,' they are given, at some length, in Galeazzi, pp. 81 *sqq.*

tance is a gratuitous gift of God means that it cannot be the result of any *natural* act upon our part, it does not mean that it cannot result from previous graces. In the case of the 'Promise' final repentance is the result of an 'efficacious' grace—a very great 'efficacious' grace.

(ii) The 'making of the Fridays' is not the cause of this great grace that is promised to the devotion, but the condition. The grace of final repentance comes from 'the exceeding great mercy' and 'all-powerful love' of the Divine Heart and is, therefore, entirely gratuitous (cf. note, p. 91).

(4) If the Promise be interpreted literally it means that Christ in His private revelations to St. Margaret Mary has established a new economy of salvation and the 'making of the Fridays' supersedes the way of salvation that is taught in public revelation.

Reply. No such conclusion may be drawn from the literal acceptance of the Promise. The ordinary economy of salvation demands for a good death either perseverance in sanctifying grace or repentance if grave sin be committed. This law remains unchanged by the Promise. But repentance requires grace—it requires 'efficacious' grace. The giving of such a grace is entirely gratuitous and God may—if He so please—attach its bestowal to the performance of some special good work. This is what He has done in the case of the 'Great Promise.' The Promise is not a substitute for perseverance in good or for repentance after sin, but is an offer to sinners—flowing from 'the exceeding great mercy' of the Sacred Heart—of a grace that will secure repentance. When Christ made through St. Margaret Mary promises of special graces and favours to those who would in different ways honour His Sacred Heart, He did not abrogate the ten commandments or change the economy of salvation, but He offered

more abundant graces for the fulfilment of the law.
The object of His promises was to draw men nearer
to Him and to make easier and more perfect the fulfilment of God's law ; and He, in His wisdom and
power, can and will secure that the object of His
promises will not be frustrated, as it would be were
men to be led into laxity rather than to greater
perfection as the result of His generosity and
mercy. The 'Great Promise' does not change the
path marked out by God to Heaven, but it offers
an additional very great grace to help towards that
goal.

(5) In Sacred Scripture justification, eternal life, is
—it would seem—promised to faith (Romans iii, 28),
to almsgiving (Tobias xii, 9), to the reception of the
Blessed Eucharist (John vi, 55). Yet we know that
such promises must be interpreted to mean that other
conditions—the general conditions of the normal
economy of salvation—must be fulfilled before the
promised favour (Justification) will be granted. Is
not the 'Great Promise' analogous ? And must it
not, therefore, be interpreted to mean that the
grace of a happy death will be granted to those who
'make the Fridays' provided they fulfil the general
conditions imposed for Justification ?

Reply. There is no analogy between the apparent
promise of salvation given in isolated passages of
Sacred Scripture and the 'Great Promise.' The
inspired books reveal to us the general economy of
salvation. When some disposition or good work is
praised or recommended in Holy Writ it is to bring
out the place which such disposition or work holds—
among others—in this general economy, not to attach
to it some special, exclusive value as the result of a
particular promise. Besides, the different parts of
S. Scripture supplement one another—and must be
interpreted in relation to one another, not in isolation

—and form with Tradition one harmonious whole, one body of doctrine. Such is not the case with the 'Great Promise'; it is complete in itself—promising clearly and definitely a certain specific grace as the result of the fulfilment of clearly defined conditions.

In any case the attribution of salvation in S. Scripture to one quality or good work is entirely apparent and is generally due to either truncated citations or mistranslations. Thus the meaning of Romans iii, 28 is not that we are justified by faith alone, but that man is justified by faith *without the works of the Law;* Tobias xii, 9 says 'for alms delivereth from death,' but adds 'and the same is that which purgeth away sins, and maketh to find mercy and life everlasting,' in other words, good works, of which almsgiving is the type, bring down mercy and mercy brings grace which secures everlasting life. As for the promise of Christ in John vi, 55, 'He that eateth my flesh and drinketh my blood hath everlasting life, and I will raise him up in the last day,' obviously it means that the Blessed Eucharist is the *principle* of resurrection and of eternal life and will lead to salvation if properly used. He does not say that he that eateth once, or so many times, or under any conditions shall receive salvation, but 'he that eateth,' i.e. he who makes this Bread his food and nourishes himself with It according to the rules established by Christ and by His Church.

There is no analogy between these general promises which, obviously, suppose certain conditions which are not explicitly mentioned and the 'Great Promise' which offers, not salvation in general, but a particular grace—the 'efficacious' grace of 'final repentance'—and that, not for the fulfilment of some vague general conditions, but for the observance of an entirely definite practice, set forth in precise terms, which do not in any way suggest that they are incomplete and presuppose other conditions.[1]

(6) To interpret the 'Great Promise' literally is to open wide the door to laxity and presumption. Having 'made the First Fridays' the sinner will consider himself free to violate the law of God because he has the assurance of the Promise that before death he will secure the grace of repentance.

Reply. If presumption of this kind were to precede or accompany the 'making of the Fridays,' it would render the fulfilment of the conditions of the 'Great Promise' impossible, for one who is prepared to violate gravely the law of God once he had 'made the Fridays' cannot worthily receive the Blessed Eucharist and so the promise of Christ no longer holds. But if such presumption should follow the due 'making of the Fridays,' what then?

(i) The 'Great Promise' is a great favour. The abuse of a favour does not destroy its use. Even the sacraments can be and are abused, but this does not impair their efficacy and utility. That a few may abuse such a great favour as the Promise embodies is no sufficient reason why many should be deprived of such an act of mercy of the Divine Heart, nor is it a cogent reason to show that such a promise cannot have been made, or, if it was, that it may not be interpreted literally.

(ii) Even if a sinner who had 'made the Fridays' were afterwards to presume on this in order to sin gravely, the 'Great Promise' would still hold. Christ can—and will—overcome by grace even such presumption. But is not the case of a person who

[1] Cf. Vermeersch, II, 140 *sqq.*

first worthily 'made the Fridays' and then resolved
to 'go to the devil,' relying on the 'Fridays,' a
purely hypothetical case ? The same God who can
give the 'efficacious' grace of repentance even to
such a one, can—and, according to our experience of
the working of Divine Providence in the domain of
grace, it is much more likely that He will *prevent*,
by His grace, such presumption, especially in the
case of one who has given proof of his sincerity in
the pursuit of salvation and who has honoured and
pleased the Sacred Heart by such a solid act of devotion as the worthy reception of the Blessed Eucharist
for nine consecutive months, and this precisely in
order to make reparation to the Divine Heart and to
secure the grace of a happy death. If Christ made the
'Great Promise' He did so—as in the case of all His
promises to St. Margaret Mary—to draw men to
Him and to make easier the way of salvation, especially
for sinners, not to open up, through gross presumption, a new road to perdition. He will, as He can,
provide against such a possible abuse of the 'Great
Promise.'

(iii) As our knowledge of the existence and meaning
of the 'Great Promise' is based on human evidence
and as no one can have *absolute* certainty that he has
duly fulfilled the conditions attaching to it, even the
literal interpretation of the Promise affords no
unassailable ground for presumption in an affair of
such supreme importance as eternal salvation. In
point of fact no evidence (as far as one can find by
experience and by careful inquiry) is forthcoming
that such presumption or laxity does in practice
result from the 'making of the Nine Fridays.' On
the contrary, we find in those who 'make the
Fridays,' heartfelt gratitude for such a favour as the
devotion promises and a realization that it is indeed a
wonderful grace flowing from 'the exceeding great

mercy ' and ' all-powerful love ' of the Heart of Jesus Christ.[1]

(iv) It is no argument against the literal interpretation of the ' Great Promise ' to say that it furnishes an occasion to sinners for laxity and presumption, for the very mercy and long-suffering of God furnish such an occasion to some sinners for obstinacy in sin and hardness of heart. Was not Christ ' set for the fall and for the resurrection of many in Israel and for a sign which shall be contradicted ' (Luke ii, 34) ; is He not for some ' a stone of stumbling and a rock of scandal ' (1 Peter ii, 8) ?

(7) If the ' Great Promise ' be accepted literally the favour which it embodies is incredible ; there is no proportion between the inestimable grace of a happy death and the reception of Holy Communion on nine consecutive first Fridays ; the grace which is offered is outside the ordinary Providence of God in reference to sinners, and is too great to be credible.

Reply. It may be quite true that there is no proportion between the grace which the Promise assures and the simple practice which secures this grace ; no such proportion is claimed, and the question of meriting the grace does not arise.[2] The ' Promise '

---

[1] To quote briefly but two writers of weight on the question of presumption, Fr. Vermeersch writes (II, 163) : ' In a rather long experience, we have not met anyone for whom the Nine Fridays has been an occasion of presumptuous temerity. The evidence of others confirms our view.' And Fr. Herbert Thurston (*The Month*, 1903, p. 649), ' With regard to the supposed assurance of salvation and consequent recklessness induced when the series of Communions has been completed, I, for one, must own myself sceptical. That a youth who has made up his mind to throw religion overboard may occasionally find it convenient to use the Nine Fridays as a retort, when his friends call him to task, may readily be understood, but that such a youth if he has any faith left, really believes his salvation to be secure, this, I think, ought not be credited except on much better evidence than I have seen yet adduced.'

[2] See pp. 99 *sqq.* above.

is, indeed, outside the ordinary economy of grace,[1] and so is described by our Lord Himself as springing from ' the exceeding great mercy ' and ' all-powerful love ' of His Heart. But our minds are not the measure of God's mercy or generosity. The chief characteristic of the entire devotion to the Sacred Heart as revealed to St. Margaret Mary is a divine mercy, a divine generosity, a divine love—that is mercy, generosity and love which know no bounds. God is master of His graces and ' no excess is incredible in the love of a God, it is only infinite excesses that are proportionate to it.'[2] To the faint-hearted Christ says, as He did to St. Margaret Mary, when she was troubled about the promulgation of devotion to His Heart, ' Dost thou not believe that I can do it ? If thou dost believe, thou shalt see the power of my Heart in the magnificence of my love.'[3] Fr. Hamon, S.J., in his *Life of St. Margaret Mary*,[4] adds these words to his account of the ' Great Promise ' : ' If we are surprised, if a promise so generous and so divine penetrates only with much difficulty into our soul, wondering, but all the while uncertain, let us read over slowly the consoling words. It is a God who expresses His will ; there is no question of merit acquired or justice to be done, it is a question of an infinite mercy that spreads itself over the world and covers it, a huge wave of love. Furthermore, are we not forewarned that the Promise is not an ordinary effect of divine love, but an excess, one of those divine interventions that fill with wondering awe men and angels. And what is more —the words of the Promise remind us—at the

---

[1] Yet not altogether, for final perseverance (and *a fortiori* final repentance) is a grace which is neither against the law (as conception without original sin is), nor above the law (as confirmation in grace is), but in accordance with the law (cf. Galeazzi, p. 220).

[2] Hamon I, 405, note 1.   [3] Cf. Hamon, I, 440.   [4] I, 434.

disposal of this excessive mercy is a love that is all-powerful, the love of the Creation, the love of the Redemption, the love of the Eucharist. . . . "Exceeding great mercy," " all-powerful love," such magnificence of language, such wealth of expression cannot clothe a commonplace promise ; in contact with divine ideas, it is wise to enlarge our own. An added hope makes brighter and more joyful life's path, thanks to the mercy of the Saviour we may chant without ceasing, " the kindness of the Lord will I evermore sing." '[1]

(8) Two minor objections are sometimes made against the practice of the devotion of the Nine Fridays (a) that in the minds of some the devotion is of more importance than the obligations of ecclesiastical, or even of divine, law (e.g. that certain persons will make zealous efforts to ' make the Fridays,' and be careless about attendance at Mass on Sundays), or that it leads to the neglect of old-established and solid practices of devotion, such as the reception of Holy Communion at Sunday Mass ; (b) that the devotion (with its insistence on *nine* Fridays, and these consecutive) smacks of the form of superstition known as 'vain observance,' and suggests such practices as ' chain-prayers' (with their emphasis on some trifling detail regarding the number of times they must be said, and their promise of very great favours, out of all proportion to the act of devotion which is performed).

Reply. (a) No practice of devotion, however solid—not even the sacraments themselves—is beyond the possibility of abuse, but ' abuse does not destroy use.' If undue importance—especially comparatively undue importance—is attached by anyone to the practice of the Nine Fridays, it will, as a rule, be due to ignorance. Such persons must be instructed in

[1] Psalm lxxxviii, 2.

the exact meaning and value of the ' Great Promise '
and its relation to the duties imposed by divine or
ecclesiastical law. Besides the conditions of the
Promise cannot be even fulfilled if essential duties
are neglected. How can persons make nine worthy
Holy Communions and honour the Sacred Heart, if
they do not intend to fulfil serious obligations ?
There is no proof that the making of the Fridays
leads to the neglect of Holy Communion on Sundays.
Quite the reverse. One of the most striking effects
of the Fridays is the promotion of frequent Holy
Communion.

(b) ' Vain observance ' is a form of superstition in
which means are used to obtain some effect which are
neither of their nature nor by ordination of God or
the Church suitable to this end, e.g. the use of charms
to cure disease or ward off evil. It is obvious that the
' making of the Fridays ' does not fall under this
description—the means which is used (the worthy
reception of Holy Communion on nine consecutive
first Fridays) is one which is calculated to lead
towards the end (a happy death), and while it would
be insufficient of itself to secure this end with certainty, it is made effective for this purpose precisely
by the promise of our Divine Lord. He may, if
He wishes, make these nine Holy Communions a
condition for the obtaining of a certain ' efficacious
grace,' which will result from them, not as a cause,
but as a condition. (The cause is the ' exceeding
great mercy,' and ' all-powerful love ' of the Heart of
Christ.)[1] He *has* made these Holy Communions such
a condition—that is precisely the meaning of the
' Great Promise.' Why He chose nine Fridays, and
not, e.g. eleven Saturdays, is His secret.[2] In point
of fact God, in His dealings with men, does prescribe
definite external practices to which He attaches

[1] Cf. note, p. 91. [2] Cf. p. 74.

I

spiritual effects—especially His grace. Such is the
nature of the sacraments themselves (though they are
causes, and not merely conditions of grace).   Christ,
in revealing the devotion to His Sacred Heart to
St. Margaret Mary, *did* teach her certain definite
practices which He desired her to adopt and to teach
to others. One of these practices is the ' making of
the Nine Fridays.'

CHAPTER IX

THE USE OF THE 'GREAT PROMISE'

IN the preceding chapters it has been shown that the evidence in favour of the historical authenticity and theological soundness of the 'Great Promise' is so satisfactory that there cannot be any reasonable doubt as to its genuine character, and it has been argued that the Promise is to be interpreted literally—its words are to be accepted in their obvious natural meaning—and that there is no cogent reason why this may not be done.

It now remains to deal with (A) the object of the 'Great Promise,' (B) the excellence of the devotion of the Nine Fridays, (C) how the 'Great Promise should be preached.

(A) *The Object of the 'Great Promise' :*

When a promise of a great reward is made it is usually in recompense for something done of great value, or because the person who promises is exceptionally generous, or because some very important end is in view. In the case of the 'Great Promise,' while recompense plays some part, it is the generosity of the one who promises and the object which is aimed at that are of importance. Our Lord is the most generous of friends. In His great love He accepts our poor efforts—themselves the fruit of His own grace—as if they were something really worth while, and He rewards them in a divine way that is with a generosity out of all proportion to the work accomplished—Godlike in its munificence. In the case of the 'Great Promise' the reward which is given is so great that it bears little or no proportion to the good works to which it is attached, and Christ Himself describes it as emanating from 'the exceeding great mercy,' and 'all-powerful love' of His Divine Heart. We cannot fathom the divine mind, nor share in the divine counsel, yet may we humbly speculate on the divine plan and see in the 'Great Promise,' a stimulus, a remedy, and an allurement.

Promises are a characteristic feature of the devotion to the Sacred Heart. They are means to an end, and the end is to draw men to the devotion, to lead them to serve God not out of fear, but out of love. The 'Great Promise' is a powerful stimulus to the practice of devotion to the Sacred Heart. It is a stimulus, too, to the frequent and regular reception of the sacraments of Penance and the Blessed Eucharist. Penance is the sovereign remedy for sin ; frequent Holy Communion is the fundamental condition of spiritual well-being as the frequent and regular taking of suitable food is an essential condition of bodily health. Our Lord in His revelations to St. Margaret Mary connected intimately the devotion to His Heart with devotion to the Blessed Eucharist in which that Heart is contained. It was in the presence of the Blessed Sacrament that the chief apparitions took place ; to receive Holy Communion in reparation was made *the* great act of the devotion and the first definite practice of it that was taught to the Saint by Christ ; it was 'during Holy Communion' that the 'Great Promise' was made. The devotion of the 'Nine Fridays' became well known about 1870, and from that time on grew and spread with quite remarkable rapidity. It broke down the rigorism, a relic of Jansenism, that then prevailed, and it seems to have been destined by Divine Providence to prepare the way for the restoration of frequent Holy Communion, and the remarkable renewal of devotion to the Blessed Sacrament which came in the opening years of the twentieth century.

The 'Great Promise' seems also to have been destined as a remedy for the evils of our day, as the general devotion to the Sacred Heart was the chief antidote to the poison of Jansenism and other ills that afflicted the Church in the eighteenth and nineteenth centuries. The chief evils of to-day are naturalism—the failure to understand and appreciate what divine grace means with the consequent neglect of the means of grace leading to spiritual ruin and eventual damnation—loss of faith manifesting itself not only by open scepticism, but more so by apathetic indifference in regard to supernatural truth, and laxity of morals bringing about general tepidity. For these grave evils the devotion of the 'Nine Fridays' provides a potent remedy. Through a realization of the love of the Sacred Heart for men, for weak and sinful men, the desire is awakened to offer Him a love of reparation in return for His love which is so little known, so much neglected and despised, and Holy Communion is worthily received regularly and perseveringly. Thus is a sense of spiritual values aroused and deepened, character is strengthened, habits of sin are broken, habits of virtue are formed, faith is enlivened, hope is renewed, love is increased. Men who will not, in an age that talks so much of liberty, be driven, are drawn by the tender, merciful, forgiving love that the 'Great Promise' proclaims, and by it Christ works sweetly yet strongly in their hearts.

The 'Great Promise' is a strong allurement. While saints eagerly follow out the divine will, the majority of men need to be attracted to its fulfilment.

The ' Great Promise ' is a promise of Christ Himself —Christ all understanding, Christ all powerful—and so for the good, who are often timid, it calms unreasonable fears about salvation, it reassures, it gives a sense of security founded on the love, liberality, mercy and power of the Divine Heart, it draws them closer to Him, it confirms and encourages them in virtue and stimulates them to ever-growing love and generosity in the divine service. For sinners the Promise has a very special attraction, to them it makes a strong appeal. Among the faithful the greater number of sinners are sinners from weakness, not from malice ; they do make efforts, perhaps many brave efforts, to serve God ; they realize the misery of sin and its disastrous consequences ; they fear the future because of their instability, and they especially dread the hour of death, lest they be then found wanting in the state of grace and lose their souls. If such sinners perish it would seem that they do so through drift and despair. To such sinners the ' Great Promise ' holds out a helping hand, it gives them a ray of hope and comfort and reassurance. They realize ' the exceeding great mercy,' the ' all-powerful love ' of the Sacred Heart ; they are drawn to confession and Holy Communion ; they come to understand the peace and joy that the service of God brings. They begin afresh, with renewed vigour, the difficult battle of life—they take up its burden with a new hope, a great vivifying hope, that, in return for the persevering efforts to make reparation to the Sacred Heart and to keep the divine law which the making of the ' Nine Fridays ' requires, Christ will come to their aid by His grace at the hour when they need Him most, the hour of death. ' They shall not die in my disfavour . . . My Divine Heart shall be their secure refuge at the last moment.' God is the master of His graces, unsearchable are His ways, on some He bestows them more lavishly than on others, for the souls of some He seems to make a special bid in His mercy. The words of the 'Great Promise' suggest that for some sinners salvation will come through the making of the 'Nine Fridays'; the 'exceeding great mercy' and 'all-powerful love' of the Sacred Heart will in their last hours come to their rescue, as He promised, and grant the grace of 'final repentance,' just because they made these Communions of reparation.

(B) *The Excellence of the Devotion of the 'Nine Fridays' :*

To receive worthily Holy Communion on nine consecutive first Fridays from love of and in reparation to the Sacred Heart is a most solid and fruitful practice of devotion. It engenders the *habit* of the reception of the sacraments. While the frequent reception of these may not mean much to the pious, it means a great deal for the sinner. To make a good confession each month for nine consecutive months means determined perseverance, it means a break with sin and sinful habits, it means the abandonment of the occasions of sin—a real reformation of life. Through familiarity it disposes of the supposed terror of the confessional and gives the sinner courage and confidence in trying to rid himself of sin. To receive Holy Communion nine times in reparation is an act most pleasing to our Divine Lord and breaks down the barrier of a false sense of unworthiness which keeps the sinner from frequently communicating. To 'make the Fridays' often, too, involves acts of real sacrifice. How many there are who travel long distances and wait even weary hours in order to get confession on the eve of the first Friday; how many who hurry fasting—perhaps a long way, and in the very early hours of the morning—to receive

Holy Communion on the first Friday before com-
mencing a hard day's work.[1]   Such sacrifices must
be most pleasing to God and consoling to Christ and
spiritually very fruitful.

Experienced priests have noted two effects of the
devotion of the Nine Fridays—(a) those who ' make
the Fridays ' do not, as a rule, stop when they have
completed the nine, they continue to go to Holy
Communion on the first Friday, generally for the
rest of their lives ; (b) the ' making of the Fridays '
has often been found to be the beginning of a new
and very different manner of life.   It has brought
home to sinners how easy, when aided by grace,
approach to Christ is and how fruitful is the regular
reception of His Body and Blood.

The devotion of the Nine Fridays is one which is
particularly in keeping with the tenor of the entire
devotion to the Sacred Heart.   That devotion was to
bring home to men the love of Christ for them and
to get them to realize the coldness and indifference
with which many treat that divine love and to seek,
therefore, from those of good will, a love of reparation.
The leading characteristic of the devotion to the
Sacred Heart is God's mercy and generosity towards
sinners ;   Christ's love for sinful men and His ardent
desire to draw them to His love, not by the rigorous
road of justice, but by the gentle way of mercy, not
by threats of punishment, but by the promise of great
rewards.

Over and over again St. Margaret Mary (especially
in her letters to her great friend and confidante,
Mother de Saumaise, and to Fr. Croiset, S.J., when
recapitulating for him the entire devotion to the

---

[1] Personally I have known artisans who went to work without
breakfast in order to be able to go to Holy Communion on the first
Friday, and persons who travelled a long distance, fasting of course,
by train in order ' not to break the Fridays.'

Sacred Heart) insists on the desire of our Lord to attract sinners and make them captive to His love, on His earnest desire to avert God's anger from sinners and ' to draw them from the path of perdition,' and secure their salvation, ' to convert the most hardened souls and to penetrate the most unfeeling hearts.'[1] She repeats that the devotion to the Sacred Heart was ' a last effort of Christ's love and mercy to draw men to Him and to draw them by the path of love.'[2] ' I am convinced,' she wrote (1689) to Sister Jeanne Madeleine Joly at Dijon, ' that He [our Lord] wishes to establish His empire by the gentleness and sweetness of His love and not by the rigour of His justice.'[3] To her brother (Chrysostom) these were her words : ' . . . the devotion to the Sacred Heart which contains treasures beyond understanding that He wishes given generously to all hearts of good will, for it is a last effort of His love towards sinners to draw them to repentance and to give them abundantly His efficacious and sanctifying graces to procure their salvation. By this means several will be drawn from the path of perdition, but woe to those who will not profit by it.'[4]

That mercy in a very special degree for sinners is a leading—if not the chief feature—of the devotion to the Sacred Heart is so fully recognized by the Church that it forms the main thought in the new liturgical formula (1929) for the Mass of the feast of the Sacred Heart, ' The designs of His Heart,' says the Introit, ' from age to age that He may save them from death, and in time of need, give them food ' (Psalm xxxii). The Collect speaks of the ' infinite treasures of love ' which God in His mercy deigns to bestow in the

---

[1] Letter CXXXII (*V.O.*, II, 557).
[2] e.g. Letters CII (*V.O.*, II, 445), CXXXIII (*V.O.*, II, 572).
[3] e.g. Letter CVIII (*V.O.*, II, 465, and cf. 462).
[4] Letter CII (*V.O.*, II, 445).

Heart of His Son. The Epistle is the passage of St. Paul's Epistle to the Ephesians (chapter iii), in which he prays that they may be able to understand ' what is the breadth, and length, and height, and depth [of the love of Christ] and to know also the charity of Christ, which surpasseth all understanding.' The words of the Gradual tell us, ' Kind and just is the Lord, therefore He giveth a law to those who might fail on the way ' (Psalm xxiv) ; while the Tract insists, ' merciful and gracious is the Lord, long-suffering and gracious, indeed ! He remaineth not angry for ever, nor doth He always chide. He dealeth not with us according to our sins, nor requiteth unto us our iniquities ' (Psalm cii). The Secret tells of the ' unspeakable love ' of the Heart of Christ ; while the Preface reminds us of the opening of our Lord's side by the lance of the soldier, ' that His Heart, that storehouse of divine bounty, being thus opened, might pour out upon us streams of compassion and grace; and fhat the Heart which has never ceased to burn with love of us might be a haven of rest for the devout; and for the penitent an open doorway to salvation.'

Now the ' Great Promise ' is but the concrete embodiment in a particular act of devotion of this mercy of the Sacred Heart towards sinners—a special effort of Christ's love to attract sinners by generosity. In return for an act of reparation to His Heart repeated perseveringly nine times He offers an immense grace—a grace which has a most special attraction for sinners—the grace of not dying in the state of mortal sin.

Of all the promises which our Lord made to St. Margaret Mary in favour of lovers of His Sacred Heart, the ' Great Promise ' is the most remarkable. It is the most concrete, definite, explicit of the promises and the favour which it embodies is a grace of supreme importance and value.

Not only is the devotion of the 'Nine Fridays' excellent in itself, but it is also excellent in its effects. As we explained above when dealing with the object of the 'Great Promise,' this practice promotes devotion to the Sacred Heart and love of God; it forms the habit of the frequentation of the sacraments; it is an antidote for the spiritual poisons of naturalism, indifference and laxity; it confirms, consoles and reassures the good; it gives comfort, hope, encouragement and healing to the sinner.

(C) *The Preaching of the 'Great Promise':*

That the 'Great Promise' should be made known far and wide is evident. In His revelations to St. Margaret Mary our Lord insisted over and over again that the treasures of grace and mercy which He opened up to her were not for herself alone, but for others. She was but 'an instrument to manifest' His love, 'an instrument to draw hearts' to Him, her heart was 'a canal' through which the riches of the Divine Heart were to flow to others, and she was to be generous and not niggardly in her distribution of this wealth.[1] 'You must not appropriate these graces,' said Christ to the Saint, 'nor be mean in distributing them to others, for I have willed to use your heart as a canal to spread them, according to my designs, in souls, many of which will by this means be drawn from the abyss of perdition.'[2] It is to men walking in the road to damnation that Christ wishes to make known 'the treasures of love, mercy, grace, sanctification and salvation,' which His Heart contains.[3] In the very letter to Mother de Saumaise in which St. Margaret Mary announces the 'Great Promise,' just before relating it, she speaks of 'the sanctifying and saving graces' which our Lord

[1] Cf. *V.O.*, I, 134, 162, 349, 460; II, 35, 193-4, 552, 582, etc.
[2] Autobiography (*V.O.*, II, 35).
[3] Letter CXXXIII, to Fr. Croiset (*V.O.*, II, 572).

ardently desires ' to communicate to souls and hearts which are well disposed.'[1] The Promise itself says it is for ' all ' who will communicate on nine consecutive first Fridays. Hence the Promise should be preached to all with courage and zeal—by word of mouth in the pulpit, in the confessional, in the schoolroom ; by writing in books and leaflets—but with knowledge, with tact and prudence. In particular it should be preached : (a) *in the spirit in which the Promise was made* by our Lord, not represented as a kind of cheap ticket or short cut to Heaven,[2] but as a singular grace, springing from ' the exceeding great mercy ' and ' all-powerful love ' of the Sacred Heart, which will lead to salutary works—to true repentance and reparation for sin—which alone can justify and save. Not by ' making the Fridays ' can a sinner claim admittance to Heaven, but through the true repentance which will justify and which will be effected by the ' efficacious ' grace which the ' making of the Fridays ' will secure ; (b) *not in isolation*, but as part of the devotion to the Sacred Heart, the whole object of which is to draw men from the path of sin and establish them firmly in a truly Christian life through love of Christ ; (c) *with simplicity and clearness*—the ordinary people have no taste for the subtilties of theology, nor have they minds trained to appreciate them ; it is not necessary to tell them about possible difficulties concerning the historical authenticity or theological soundness of the ' Great Promise,' but it is very important to make clear to them what the Promise really is, how and why they should fulfil its conditions ; and they should understand its real value,

---

[1] Letter LXXXVI (*V.O.*, II, 397).

[2] To ' make the Fridays ' with the idea that the devotion is a short cut to heaven would be to run the risk of not fulfilling the conditions of the Promise. To communicate worthily one must intend to persevere in God's service and lead a truly Christian life.

and that while we have moral certainty about its origin and meaning, we have not the absolute certainty that is proper to the truths of public revelation. It would be well, too, that intelligent Catholics should realize that the Church cannot officially guarantee the authenticity or exact interpretation of the Promise and why this is so.

Résumé.

In many apparitions during her life as a nun (1672–1690) in the Visitation Monastery of Paray-le-Monial, our Lord taught St. Margaret Mary Alacoque the principles and practices of the devotion to the Sacred Heart in the form in which it has been recognized and accepted by the Church. He made her many promises in favour of those who would practise the devotion. One of these is known as the 'Great Promise,' in which our Lord promises to all who will receive Holy Communion on nine consecutive First Fridays of the month the grace of final repentance. This promise was announced by St. Margaret Mary in a letter to her former superior, Mother de Saumaise, written between 1687 and 1689. The original letter is not extant, but we have trustworthy and very early copies of it, whose authenticity and correctness are accepted by those who are competent to pass judgement on the question. The words of the Promise are to be accepted as they stand—according to their natural, obvious meaning—unless cogent arguments are advanced to show that they may not be thus understood. No such arguments have, in fact, been advanced. The meaning, then, of the 'Great Promise' is that to those who communicate worthily on nine consecutive first Fridays of the month our Lord promises an '*efficacious*' grace which will secure that they shall die in the state of grace, in His friendship, and have His Heart as their assured refuge in their last hours.   Hence the ' Great Promise ' affords *moral certainty of salvation* for those who duly fulfil the conditions which it embodies— but as our knowledge of the giving of the Promise, of the correctness of its form, of the meaning to be attached to it, are all based on human though unimpeachable evidence, and not divinely guaranteed, and as no one can be *absolutely* certain that he has duly fulfilled its conditions, the ' Great Promise ' gives not absolute and infallible certainty of salvation, but moral certainty.   This, according to Catholic teaching, is, indeed, the only certainty of salvation that we can have, apart from special revelation.

INDEX[1]

[1] The names of authors are given in italics.

Charles Birchall & Sons Ltd. London & Liverpool.